José Silva

José Silva

The Man
Who Tapped the Secrets
of the Human Mind
and
the Method He Used

Robert B. Stone, Ph.D.

H J Kramer Inc
Tiburon, California

Many thanks go to José Silva, for making this book possible;
to my wife, Lola, for serving as sounding board;
and to Dawn Schwirtz,
for transforming a manual into a manuscript.
R.B.S.

H J Kramer Inc
P.O. Box 1082
Tiburon, CA 94920

Library of Congress Cataloging-in-Publication Data

Stone, Robert B.
    José Silva : the man who tapped the secrets of the human mind /
Robert B. Stone.
        p.   cm.
    Includes bibliographical references.
    ISBN 0-915811-29-4 : $9.95
    1. Silva, José, 1914–   . 2. Silva Mind Control. 3. Teachers—
United States—Biography. 4. Inventors—United States—Biography.
5. Authors—United States—Biography. I. Title.
BF1127.S54S76   1990
158'.9—dc20
[B]   90-52705
                                                                  CIP

Cover Design: Spectra Media
Typesetting: Classic Typography
Book Production: Schuettge & Carleton
Assistant Editor: Nancy Grimley Carleton
Manufactured in the United States of America
10 9 8 7 6 5 4 3 2 1

Dedication

To the Higher Intelligence
to which all human minds are connected.

To Our Readers
The books we publish are our
contribution to an emerging world based
on cooperation rather than on competition, on
affirmation of the human spirit rather than on self-
doubt, and on the certainty that all humanity is
connected. Our goal is to touch as many
lives as possible with a message
of hope for a better world.
Hal and Linda Kramer,
Publishers

Contents

Preface

As the author or coauthor of some seventy-five self-help books, I have written several biographies of individuals who have been a special inspiration to others. These subjects have included the head of what was the largest publishing house in the world when the book was written, a star in his realm; a four-star general, the youngest ever to receive the distinction; and a woman who starred in the entertainment field.

The man who is the subject of this book is a star in the field of evolution, the evolution of mankind. If you think this is too tall an order for one individual to fill, read on.

You will experience two major benefits as you read this book. First, you will discover how one man harnessed scientific and spiritual powers to develop a method to use more of the mind, and how he used those powers heroically to overcome scientific and spiritual opposition. And, second, you will acquire insight into and a practical understanding of the Silva Mind Control Method for enhancing your own quality of life.

José Silva, founder of this method, never had a day of formal schooling in his life. At the age of six, he was the family breadwinner, selling newspapers and shining shoes. He went on to become a successful businessman, an inventor, and an electronics specialist. In this amazing range of accomplishments, he resembles another man who had little formal schooling, the late Walter Russell. As a physicist, Russell codiscovered heavy water, which ushered in the atomic age. Russell was also an architect of buildings in New York City, the sculptor of two presidents, and much more. The author of a biography of Russell called his book *The Man Who Tapped the Secrets of the Universe*. This inspired the subtitle of my biography of José Silva, *The Man Who Tapped the Secrets of the Human Mind*.

At the age of seventy-six, José Silva is obviously doing more than making discoveries. Yes, he is tapping the computerlike capacity of the brain to raise the intelligence measured in IQ tests, but he is also activating the creative power of human beings, interpreting ancient teachings in light of New Age thinking, and giving humankind the hope that it may someday empty the prisons, hospitals, and battlefields of the world.

I have been a lecturer on the Silva Method for more than fifteen years, and as such have come to wish I could shout from the rooftops its many quiet successes—the slow advent of first psychoneuroimmunology and then cyberphysiology in the medical field, the accomplishments of entire faculties in the education field based on the Silva Method, and the secret problem-solving achievements of business executives who use the method daily.

This book may be my rooftop. But it is also your foundation—for starting the great new life that comes with an elevated awareness of the human potential and a method to activate it.

> *Robert B. Stone, Ph.D.*
> Kaneohe, Hawaii
> 1 July 1990

Part I
José Silva

Chapter 1
The Man, the Message, and the Method

Many life stories are told only after their subjects have died. José Silva is very much alive and, as unbelievable as it may seem, is likely to have become even more so by the time you have this book in your hands.

The reason for this is that the spark of life is fanned by creativity, and José Silva is training ordinary people to be geniuses. And not just on a hit-or-miss basis but with a 100 percent batting average. It does not matter who decides to take the training in the Silva Method — young or old, rich or poor, stupid or smart, Eastern or Western, black or white, Catholic or Muslim, illiterate or educated. In every student of the training, the IQ goes up, the health improves, problems are solved, personal effectiveness soars, creativity is enhanced, intuition becomes more dependable, and life itself gets better and better.

Although you may have heard of José and even of the Silva Mind Control Method, it is likely that you know little about either one. And if it were not for this book, you would probably learn little more about the man or the method for a long, long time. The reason for this is that most earlier books have not delved deeply into the man or the method, and those people who have taken the training generally keep very quiet about it; they know few would believe them if they described what they had experienced.

But there is no secret about this body of knowledge. Students are not exhorted to hush it up. Nevertheless, its effects remain in the realm of the unbelievable: The method steps up practitioners' control of their minds to the point where they are able to function mentally in incredible ways — ways that are not taught in school, ways that are frequently indescribable verbally, and ways that scientists are only now beginning to understand.

If you saw a UFO, would you talk about it? Probably not. You might be afraid that if you did people would think you were crazy. It's somewhat like that with the Silva Method. A graduate who gets up the nerve to tell his neighbors might have to say good-bye to neighborhood barbecues. Even a wife might alienate her husband, or a husband his wife. Only when the graduate actually demonstrates dramatic accomplishments does the familiar "Oh, yeah?" give way to fascination.

Meanwhile, education plays hide-and-seek with the Silva Method. It gives lip service to restructuring, innovation, and community input while hiding from all three behind a barrier called "tried and true."

The medical profession plays a similar game. It recognizes that help from the mind in curing the body is possible. It even lends its terminology to such a relationship, offering the words *cyberphysiology* and *psychoneuroimmunology*. Nevertheless, the medical community as a whole leans away from inquiries into the mind-body link and toward the more lucrative approaches the chemical industry provides.

The government, too, avoids this great problem-solving tool. The bigger its avowed fight against drugs and crime, the bigger those problems seem to become. But it turns its back on such solutions as the Silva Method.

The fact that José Silva has never had a day of formal education in his life and yet is the trainer of geniuses makes him unique. As you turn the pages ahead, more unique aspects of his life will unfold in the form of one-in-a-billion coincidences, serendipities, and "lucky breaks." You will sense, as I do, that a higher intelligence has been "pulling the strings" regarding the development of José's work.

In the process of reading about the man, his message, and his method, you will become privy to his techniques for achieving "unattainable" goals and triggering breakthrough solutions to "unsolvable" problems. In this respect, the book is a how-to volume as well as a biography. It will teach you how to transform your mind into a supermind by plugging into the very source of intelligence itself—using as a model a man who had something special going for him right from the start. Gradually, as you read, pictures of the man and his method will clarify and illuminate each other. In those clear images, you will discern José Silva's mission.

As José worked with his ten children as they acquired their education, he laid the groundwork for the potential-releasing method that is taught worldwide today. In 1966, he gave up a lucrative electronics business to launch the Silva Method commercially. He had first offered the Silva Method to several branches of the federal government, realizing that his unexpected successes at deepening intelligence belonged more appropriately in Washington, D.C., than in Laredo, Texas. In each case, the reply was "Don't call us, we'll call you."

Today, Silva Mind Control International, Inc., employs fifty people in Laredo. The center's employees print the manuals, newsletters, and brochures; assemble biofeedback equipment; and oversee the four hundred–odd lecturers in some seventy-nine countries that give the training in sixteen languages.

José Silva lives in an adjacent house with his wife, Paula. His ten children are adults and have among them twenty-seven children of their own. Though his work to awaken genius has already benefited some ten million people, José remains a family man who places his wife, children, and other relatives foremost while he attunes his mind to a higher intelligence, making this a better world for all to live in.

White-haired and vigorous at age seventy-six, José teaches advanced courses for graduates at the center. He also travels extensively, lecturing worldwide. His audiences frequently exceed the one thousand figure.

What is it that these millions of Silva Method graduates actually learn, and how can it change the world? Modern physics is beginning to postulate that there must be a field of intelligence in space in order to explain what is observed in the laboratory. That field of intelligence, first called the collective unconscious by Dr. Carl Jung, is now given more scientific names, such as the morphogenetic field. And controversy is building between the classical Newtonian scientists and the New Age Einsteinian scientists. José Silva teaches how to tap into this larger intelligence for everyday solutions and benefits.

His is a rags-to-riches story in the Horatio Alger tradition. José accomplished more as an unschooled lay scientist than many a multidegreed professional. José's system to awaken the genius within has already benefited some ten million people and is still spreading to reach more.

Some excerpts from recent newspapers reveal the need for what José has to offer:

"American schools are graduating students who lack even the skills needed to fill existing assembly-line jobs, let alone the sophisticated new jobs that increasingly dominate the economy."

"[Our schools have] the makings of a national disaster."

"A Third World [is growing] within our own country."

"The American dream [has] turned into a nightmare."

"A fourth of high school students drop out and another fourth don't come close to having the skills to survive.... "

These statements were all made at a conference of the nation's governors convened to confront the fact that industry in the United States is facing a catastrophe because schools are failing to educate students.

The Silva Method has been used by a few educators—only a few, because it does not conform to the standard approach, and it has been created by an "outsider." The few school administrators who have permitted faculty members and/or student bodies to be trained in the method have been largely private schools,* which are often more flexible than public institutions. In some cases, standardized psychological tests were administered before and after the training to gauge the results. Despite the fact that the benefits went far beyond the factors that the tests were constructed to measure, here are some of the results:

In high school students who took the training, strong changes were recorded in the direction of ego strength, maturity, calmness, and the facing of reality. A follow-up study showed that these changes were lasting and indeed increased over a period of time.

*The Silva Mind Control Courses: Effects With Three High School Populations (Laredo, Texas: SMCI, 1974).

Adult graduates have shown

1. a decrease of inhibitions in social interactions;
2. a movement away from states described as "tense, frustrated, and overwrought," and toward those described as "relaxed, tranquil, and composed."
3. A shift away from "apprehensive, troubled, worrying" and toward "self-assured, placid, serene."

Personality improvements, whether in students or in adults, generate gains in effectiveness, in turn yielding better student learners and more successful adult producers. Enhanced self-concept is the key.

How can a man who was neither educated nor trained as an educator produce a training that could soon prove to be the salvation for the educational system? The answer is no more rooted in logic than is the training itself. Rather, it is linked to the generally untapped relationship between the rational and the intuitive aspects of the mind.

The rational aspect of the mind is the foundation for standard education as it stands today. The intuitive aspect, however, is almost totally ignored by standard education. The Silva Method exposes this oversight as humanity's single most serious error.

Graduates of this Silva Method are sure of this. By the time you finish reading this book, you should be, too.

The Silva Method is a concise methodology designed to give you what education and experience in this material world fail to deliver. On the surface, the results of the training appear to be improved memory, increased control over unwanted habits and desired skills, increased problem-solving ability, improved health, increased self-confidence, and an enhanced level of creativity and intuition.

Beneficial as these results are, the training offers more and goes farther. In fact, the extra distance it goes takes it out of the reach of our vocabulary, which has been structured for this material world, not for the creative realm from which the material world springs. The Silva Method moves its trainees in the direction of this creative realm.

The creative realm is intelligence, pure and simple. There, in the creative realm, all is clarity. The complication lies in the *created* realm, where we get lost in its maze of complexity. Getting lost in this maze can kill us. The Silva Method enables us to reconnect with the creative realm in order to come alive.

Today, as the beneficiaries of the training reach the ten million mark, the man who created it is convinced that more and more Silva lecturers will mean accelerated inroads into institutionalized education, business, industry, and perhaps even into the religious establishment. The lecturers are the method's messengers, linking ever greater portions of the human family with the creative source.

Who becomes a Silva lecturer? Typically, graduates who are so impressed with the personal changes the Silva Method has brought about in their own lives that they dedicate themselves to sharing it with others. Once a graduate makes that commitment, he or she takes an intensive two-week training in Laredo.

What personal changes spur such a commitment? Consider Gerald Seavey's answer to this question. When he signed up for training in the Silva Method, he had a two-hundred-dollar-a-day heroin addiction. He heard his lecturer say, "Change the unwanted habit programming at the cause level and you change behavior at the effect level."

Skeptical, but with a glimmer of hope, Seavey began to relax daily and to see himself differently in his imagination.

"Three times a day, I programmed that by July 20, which was thirty days from the date of my initial programming, all desire for heroin would disappear forever. During the thirty days, I continued to use drugs but slowly decreased the amount I used, pacing myself so I would be off heroin completely by my target date.

"On that great day in July, I stopped using heroin and have never used it since. It was not at all like the many times before, when I stopped using drugs only to return to them a few days or weeks later. This time it was my gut feeling that I genuinely had no desire for heroin. No willpower was required, no suppressing of feelings and desires. It worked! I was free at last!"

That blessing motivated Seavey to share the method in Boston, where he has trained thousands over the past twenty years.

Betty Perry, of Florida, is another graduate turned lecturer:

"In 1980 I weighed over 170 pounds, had limitations in the use of my left hand, had no peripheral vision to the left, and had a terrible memory and worse attitude. Since 1966, I had believed the doctors when they told me I was lucky to have survived the stroke I had that year and to remember that I had brain damage. But in 1980 a Silva lecturer was telling me I could do something about it. What did I have to lose?

"I used a very active and funny series of visualizations. I had plumbers and electricians repairing the brain damage. Blood vessels were pipes the plumbers could fix. Nerves were wires the electricians worked on with the help of electronic engineers, who reprogrammed the computer. In the white-framed mirror of my mind, I imagined myself free of the physical limitations that had been part of my life for fourteen years.

"Within three months, there were definite improvements, and they increased until now only a neurologist can detect any limitations in my physical functioning. But that was only the beginning. Once I was better physically, I began to look for other ways to improve my life. I can honestly say that I am healthier, happier, and more successful now than at any other time in my life."

My own motivation to become a Silva lecturer occurred on still another level of consciousness. After researching, teaching, and writing on the powers of the mind for decades, I was team teaching self-hypnosis with a physician at a commercial class at Waikiki's famous Ilikai Hotel. While taking a break, I was attracted by another lecturer's voice in a room across the hall. What that fellow was describing sounded a little like self-hypnosis. I looked at the card on the meeting room door. It read, "SILVA MIND CONTROL." I stood stock-still outside the door, listening. The lecturer was making such statements as these:

"Geniuses use more of their mind and use it in a special manner. You are now learning to use more of your mind and to use it in a special manner."

"Every time you function at these levels of mind, you will receive beneficial effects physically and mentally."

"You will always maintain a perfectly healthy body and mind."

I returned to eavesdrop again later, and heard references this time to healing others, communicating subjectively with other people over vast distances, ordering and getting valuable information in a dream, and taking part in constructive and creative activities to improve the world. The applications of self-hypnosis are fairly well limited to improving self-image, gaining self-confidence, and getting rid of unwanted habits. This Silva Mind Control business sounded head and shoulders above that.

I took the training, and it was a blockbuster. I informed the physician I was working with that I was quitting, and within a year I was a certified Silva lecturer.

But this is not an autobiography. It is the story of the man whose method rocked the medical world, injected a new dimension into the business world, provided athletes with ways of developing superhuman powers, and today promises to jolt all of humanity into a spiritual awakening.

It is important to keep in mind that José Silva did not start out with the development of this method as his goal. Under the expert eye of its earthly human creator, it seemed to sprout and evolve of its own accord.

The key to the method is the right hemisphere of the brain. The Silva Mind Control Method was launched and underway for nearly a decade before José understood the significance of the brain's right hemisphere. Instead of referring to the left and right hemispheres, therefore, the training talks about objective and subjective mental functioning. We now know that objective mental functioning is characteristic of the left brain, and subjective mental functioning is characteristic of the right brain.

José had been aware of the distinction between subjective and objective mental functioning since childhood, and this single perception enabled him to be in the right place at the right time with the right idea time after time. These opportunities occurred too frequently for them to be ascribed to "luck" or "coincidence." They themselves proved the value of the method.

Most people hear about the Silva Mind Control Method in

the newspapers. A Silva lecturer advertises a free lecture at a
local hotel or motel. Shall we go in?

As we enter, we are handed an attendance card to fill out and
some leaflets and brochures. When the free lecture begins, we
settle back to listen to the speaker discuss one of the most in-
triguing subjects possible—the human brain.

José Silva used to to do the lectures regularly, but now he
leaves it to the lecturers and confines his public-speaking activities largely to advanced aspects of the method. In this instance,
the lecturer has greeted his audience and summarized the ground
he will cover, and is now explaining a chart on the wall labeled
"Scale of Brain Evolution." He explains that the chart is a map
illustrating our concepts about the body, brain, and mind. The
chart is divided both horizontally and vertically. The left side
represents the body; the center section, the brain; the right
side, the mind. The train track with the numbers is a measurement scale for the brain's vibration rate.

The lecturer then introduces a scientific concept fundamental to the Silva Mind Control Method: that the human brain
vibrates, much as the heart beats, but more rapidly. The heart
beat is measured in times per minute, but the brain vibrates so
many times per *second*. Further, the rate of vibration varies with
the mental level being experienced.

The average vibration for a person who is wide awake is normally about twenty vibrations, or cycles, per second. Anything
over fourteen cycles per second is called beta brain activity. Beta
activity is associated with the outer world of the body. It takes
place when we are using our physical senses and are conscious
of time and space. This relates to an outer, conscious level of
mind.

Slower vibrations, between seven and fourteen cycles per second, are known as alpha brain waves. This level is associated
with dreams—both dreams in sleep and daydreams. Frequencies between four and seven cycles per second are called theta
brain waves. Alpha and theta are not involved with the physical world and physical senses; when we are experiencing them
we are not necessarily aware of time and space. In this dimension, we can use our intuition, our subjective senses, to obtain

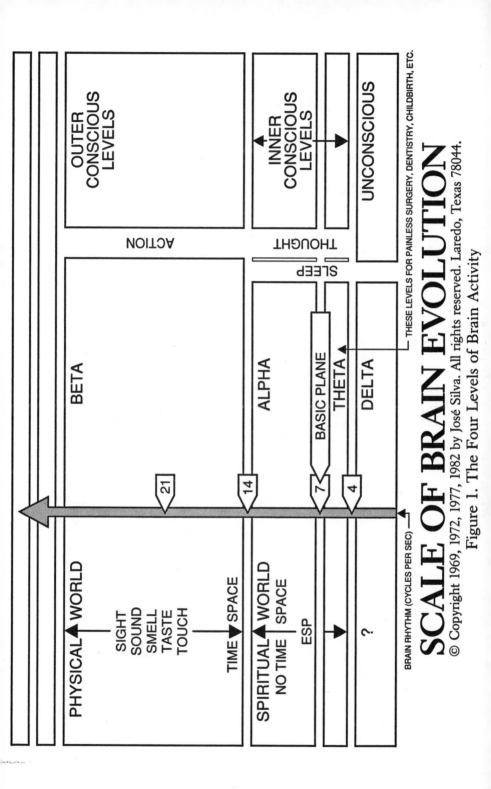

SCALE OF BRAIN EVOLUTION

Figure 1. The Four Levels of Brain Activity

information that will help us accomplish our goals. The theta waves are associated with an *inner* conscious level of mind, what psychologists might call the subconscious level. But this level is not "sub-" to us; we are able to use it consciously to make changes.

The lowest frequencies, which we reach during deep sleep, are called delta wave frequencies, below four cycles per second. It is said that few people are able to remember information when their brains are vibrating at delta levels. Little is known about delta at this time, which accounts for the question mark on the chart.

Notice that the chart is called the Scale of Brain Evolution. Scientists tell us that the human brain developed over millions of years, and that levels functioning at higher and higher frequencies evolved, with the beta level the highest known level to date. This process of evolution is repeated in every human embryo, with the first detectable frequencies being delta. Once the brain has reached today's state of evolution, the infant is born. The child functions in delta more than any other frequency until four years old, confirmed in our experience by how much babies and young children sleep.

As children grow, they begin to use more of their brains, a fact evidenced by faster frequencies. From four to seven years old, children function mostly in the theta levels when their eyes are closed. At about the time the baby teeth fall out and the permanent teeth come in, there is a shift in brain functioning. Now alpha frequency is detectable when the eyes are closed, the right side of the brain begins to be used more, and the child becomes more imaginative and a more rapid learner. When the eyes are focused, the brain functions at beta, usually at twenty cycles.

The time at which this shift occurs is critical. If the child is taught at this point to use both the left and right brain hemispheres for thinking, he or she will retain that valuable ability throughout life. Unfortunately, few people learn to use both hemispheres. Instead, for most people, overall average brain-wave frequency increases as development proceeds, thinking with the right brain decreases, and ultimately about ninety percent of humanity grows to use the left brain hemisphere alone in its thinking.

At this point in the Silva Method introductory presentation, the lecturer will attach the electrodes of a small electronic gadget onto his or her fingers, explaining that this is a biofeedback device that indirectly indicates brain-wave frequency. When the device is turned on, a pulsing sound is audible. The demonstrator will tune it to a faster beat.

"Listen to what happens when I close my eyes and take a deep breath," says the lecturer.

Immediately the pulsing rate slows. When the lecturer opens his eyes, the pulse speeds up again.

"When I closed my eyes and took a deep breath," the lecturer explains, "I was relaxing. A relaxed person has a lower electrical conductivity in the skin. This device measures changes in skin conductivity and records these changes audibly. Skin conductivity isn't important in itself, but its changes parallel changes in brain-wave frequency. So what this machine was actually indicating indirectly was a slowing of my brain waves."

When we relax and slow our brain-wave frequency to the alpha range—seven to fourteen vibrations per second—we are at the center of our frequency range. This is where both brain hemispheres, not just the left, take part in the thinking process. With the right hemisphere participating, you are a different person than when only the left hemisphere is involved in thinking: You are wiser, you have a higher IQ, you are able to be more creative, and you are able to solve problems that would ordinarily stymie you.

Very simply put, the Silva Method is a way of voluntarily entering the alpha level. Once there, you are able to use more of your mind, and your mind controls your brain. The brain itself is similar to a giant computer. With your mind in alpha, you can "program" that computer to change old thought and feeling patterns and to reach the goals you yearn for in the future.

Although the standard introductory lecture brings to light the main thrust of the training—learning to function at the relaxed, alpha level of mind—two aspects of alpha functioning give the story of José's progress toward discovering them more suspense and excitement.

The first is the cybernetic notion of the human brain as a computer. José was pushed into electronics "by coincidence." Had he not been, he would undoubtedly have taken a much longer time to succeed in his first amateurish research into the mind.

The three pounds of matter that we call the brain contains some thirty billion neurons. A neuron is a collection of molecules that act together to process and store information. Each can be compared to a circuit in a computer.

In itself, the idea that we all have a computer inside our heads with the equivalent of thirty billion circuits is absolutely awesome. However, since every atom making up those neurons is contributing to our intelligence, it is not the thirty billion figure, but rather the total number of atoms, some one hundred trillion trillion, that represents the limit of our potential brain power!

One hundred trillion trillion—now, that's a difficult concept to get a handle on. Imagine yourself sitting in an average-size living room and that each atom in your brain is a BB gun pellet. Suppose you have one hundred trillion trillion of these tiny pellets and wanted to fill up your living room with them. Would you have enough?

Yes, you would, with plenty left over. Suppose you also filled up your neighbor's living room. Yes, still plenty left over. Suppose that every second you filled up another living room.

Now snap your fingers once a second until all the pellets are used up. Do you know how long you would be snapping your fingers? Some twenty million years.

Does it occur to you that your own brain might be short a few neurons? Or that the next guy has more than you? Forget it. The only problem is that you are using only a fraction of these thirty million brain neurons. José Silva devoted his energy to figuring out how you might use more.

But that's only half the story. José also saw, in a flash of genius that eluded other students of the brain, the deep significance of the right hemisphere. This second exciting aspect of his discovery is an ancient secret of the human mind. We have long understood that the left side of the brain ran the right side of the body and that the right side of the brain ran the left side of the body. We also knew that should one side of the brain be injured, the other side would act as a backup system and come to its support.

But early research into the hemispheres of the brain ran into one formidable block: owing to the connectedness of the two sides of the brain, scientists could not differentiate between left and right brain functioning. The connection was sometimes severed in mentally ill patients, and in them the distinction between types of brain functioning was clearer. But these were not normal subjects, so the research could not be generalized to the rest of us.

Then it was discovered that one hemisphere could be anesthetized and effectively put out of action while the other remained unaffected. From that research, it was discovered that we live in a left-brain world: The left side, which is called the left brain, is interested in the exterior, material environment and involved in activity, motion, logical thinking, and the understanding of time and space.

The right brain was revealed to have a different perspective. Its interest was more internal than external. It was passive and meditative. It preferred to guide its thinking by feelings and hunches. It was creative, intuitive, and instinctive.

The right-brain viewpoint seemed out of step with "reality" — that is, with the material world. This explains why the right brain and its functions have virtually been ignored by conventional methods of education, since the purpose of those methods has been to prepare us to survive in this material world.

Similarly, the right brain has never figured prominently in our modes of conducting government, international relations, politics, business, or even health care — since all these aspects of our lives have been relegated solely to the material world. As a result, all these areas of human existence have largely been deprived of the right-brain intelligence, an intelligence that appears to be anchored *behind* the material creation.

José Silva perceived the supreme importance of fathoming and using that intelligence in daily life. He did so because *in him* both sides of his brain were functioning fully.

What was there about José's early life that kept his right brain from decreasing in function, as has been the general pattern for the rest of us? And how did he tap the secret of the human mind?

For that answer, we need to start at the beginning.

Chapter 2
Six-Year-Old Entrepreneur

José Silva was born on August 11, 1914, at 2:14 A.M. in Laredo, Texas, in the house where his mother, Isabel, had been born.

Although her home was in Monterrey, Mexico, Isabel went to Laredo, where her mother lived, every time she was about to give birth to a child, so that the child would be an American citizen. When José was born, she had already had two girls—one died before José was born, leaving Josefina the sole girl. Two more boys were to come—Juan, younger than José by two years, and Albert, younger by four years.

Isabel returned to Monterrey with her new baby. These were the years of the Mexican Revolution. A day did not pass without soldiers marching through Monterrey. Frequently, soldiers would stop to rest and ask for water. Isabel refused to come out of the house with soldiers around, so little José brought water to them.

José's father, also named José, worked on the Mexican railroad, as did most of the other male members of the family. The railroad tracks were only a block behind the Silva house, and José senior would hop off the train there after work and walk home. José always rushed to meet him halfway when he heard the train, eager for the fruit or candy his father always brought him.

Next, the tired railroad man would take off his jacket and shirt, sit down on the back steps leading into the kitchen where his wife Isabel was preparing dinner, and invite José to scratch his back. He really enjoyed that.

Train wrecks were common during the revolution, as railroad bridges were frequently blown up. José senior survived many wrecks, but during one his foot was caught in the wreckage and boiling water from the engine poured over him. "I remember visiting him in the hospital," recalled José. "A nurse wheeled him to the hospital porch. He was totally covered with white ointment and gauze. As soon as the outside air blew on him, he fainted and they wheeled him back into the hospital again. That memory kept alive a question in my mind for many years. What

17

happened to him—where did he go and what did he do when he fainted?"

José's father survived, but he was in such a weak state when he left the hospital that when an influenza epidemic hit Mexico in 1918, he was one of the first to succumb.

At the time of his death, Isabel was pregnant with Albert, so after the funeral the family returned to Laredo, this time to live with José's grandmother. Though pregnant, Isabel Silva went to work as a clerk in a dry goods store, since the only other wage earner in the family was her brother Manuel, who had accompanied them there. After Albert was born, she returned to that job while José's grandmother took care of the children.

Isabel had been married at the age of fourteen, and even after having five children she was still a beautiful woman. Following her bereavement, the young widow started to receive offers of marriage and soon accepted a divorced machinist twenty years her senior. José's new stepfather and his mother moved to another Texas city to work, taking with them Juan, age three. But José's grandmother insisted that José and his older sister, Josefina, remain with her. An aunt whose family was all grown up and who loved the baby, Albert, asked to have him. Albert lived with her until he was fourteen years old.

A mother bear teaches her cubs to climb a tree when there is danger and to stay in the tree until she calls them down. Then, one day, she gives the danger signal, and with the cubs in the tree she takes off for good. So it was with Isabel.

Now José's grandmother became José's mother and his Uncle Manuel became his father.

The loss of a parent is always a moving experience for a young child. Looking back some seventy years after his father's death and his mother's disappearance, José sees this period as the time when he began wondering about life. Why were these things happening? "I thought about things a five-year-old does not usually consider," he mused. "I wondered, what's going on, why am I here, why are we in one person's life and not in somebody else's?"

There is something to be said for the strengthening effect the loss of both parents can have on a child. It is certainly true that parental love and a coherent family unit are important ingredients in wholesome growth. But when they are withdrawn, certain youngsters may respond to the challenge in a positive and meaningful way.

When José was six, his Uncle Manuel worked in a steam laundry about a block away from the house. Two blocks away was another building that was owned by a British smelting company. Josefina had been enrolled in a small private school. Since José was not old enough to attend, and since things were tough financially, Uncle Manuel made José a shoeshine box so he could make some extra money at the laundry and the smelter.

Shining shoes was fun. José enjoyed the smiles he received from his customers when he finished their shoes. He also enjoyed contributing money to his grandmother's household expenses. He decided he could do more. He began selling newspapers. Some customers bought a shoeshine *and* a newspaper; some bought one or the other. Uncle Manuel helped José prepare separate lists of those who wanted just newspapers, just shoeshines, or both. Entered there were each customer's name and address or office number as well as the dates when he wanted either or both services. These lists helped José give his customers what they wanted when they wanted it.

Although he did not realize it at the time—he was only six!—José was already garnering experiences that would serve him well for the rest of his life. He was learning to use the logical left side of the brain for record-keeping activities along with the creative, intuitive right side of the brain to serve his customers better and come up with imaginative ideas for earning more money. In this regard, he was placing himself in the top ten percent of the world's people—all largely left-brained individuals.

The pennies and nickels added up. Soon José was making a dollar a day, which was what most adults in his world were earning. But his business kept on growing—and soon he had reached two dollars a day, more than Uncle Manuel was making. By the time José was seven, school age, he was contributing to the family on a par with his uncle. Since the family was struggling financially, it was decided that José would continue working instead of going to school.

Soon he added a third activity to his business—distributing the circulars that grocery stores handed out on Sundays to advertise their prices.

One day while shining shoes at the British smelting company, José began to imagine what the offices inside the building looked like. Then his curiosity took him a step farther. Did the people working in those offices have to clean their own offices after closing time? he wondered. When the general manager stopped by for a shoeshine, José acted on the mental image he had conjured up.

"Sir, how would you like me to clean your office after closing?"

The man looked down at him. There was interest in his eyes. "How much would you want for doing that?" he asked.

"Whatever you think it is worth."

"I'll try you out for one week."

José arrived at the manager's office promptly at closing time. He was asked to sweep, dust, oil the furniture, and clean the windows. He also decided to empty the pencil sharpener, install paper rolls in the toilet, and mop the floor. He finished by getting all the trash out of the office and placing it outside for pickup by the trash collector.

In the days that followed, he found a five dollar bill on the floor and a watch sitting on the desk. He knew intuitively that he was being tested. He put these items in a drawer and the next day told the manager what he had found and where he had put them.

Looking back, José recalled, "I didn't understand how I was functioning mentally until decades later, when I was researching the human mind. I was using both brain hemispheres—the logical left and the intuitive right. I was becoming a naturally developed clairvoyant, able to project my ideas to people to help them sense I was honest in my dealings. And I'm sure this helped me to sense their needs better as well."

This first week of office cleaning was so successful that José was assigned to clean other offices at a fee per office. Now he was cleaning offices at night, shining shoes and selling newspapers on weekdays, and delivering grocery circulars on Sundays. By the time he was nine and ten, he had added grass cutting and gardening to his work program. He was now the main provider in the family and saving money to boot.

When he was twelve, José learned to drive his uncle's Model T Ford. That provided him with another money-making opportunity: Once a month, he drove a wealthy lady around town to collect her rents.

Other business ventures came and went in those early teen years, but when he was seventeen, José got an idea that stood out in his mind as something he had to do. He wanted to drive to San Antonio, buy merchandise at wholesale that could not be obtained in Laredo, and return to sell it in Laredo.

San Antonio is 150 miles north of Laredo. The highway was then unpaved and by no means an all-weather road—some sections were hard surface, but there were many sandy sections. José's first step was to engineer Uncle Manuel's consent to use the new Model A Ford—a four-door car with a removable canvas top, canvaslike curtains with snap-on buttons, and small celluloid windows for protection against the rain.

"It's not the car. It's the distance," warned Uncle Manuel, in doubt about the scheme. "You should take somebody with you."

"How about Beto?" José suggested. Beto was José's eleven-year-old cousin, and like a brother to him.

His grandmother entered the conversation. "Beto is too young for such a trip and so are you," she argued. "You have never driven that far before. You have plenty to do in Laredo. Why must you go to San Antonio and take such chances?"

"I have a business idea I want to try out," explained José.

"Mind your Laredo business. It keeps you busy. And anyway, what kind of business?" his grandmother asked.

José paused. He did not want to go into too much detail. In fact, he was not sure exactly what products would be available in San Antonio. "Buy wholesale there and sell the stuff here," he said.

"What nonsense." She threw up her hands and walked out of the room.

José withdrew much of his savings for expenses and the purchase of inventory. It took him and Beto a full day of driving to reach San Antonio—from before daybreak to after dark. His

mother was now living in San Antonio, so they went to her house
to spend the night. This gave him a chance to see his brother
Juan and his sister Josefina, both of whom were living with Isabel
at the time. Everyone was amazed that the boys had driven all
the way from Laredo that day.

The next morning, José and Beto left early for the wholesale
merchandise area. They found exactly the type of articles José
had hoped to buy: combs, buttons, sewing needles, spools of
black and white thread, shoe polish, shoelaces, thimbles, bottles of hair tonic and hair oil, fingernail cutters and files, and
handkerchiefs.

The prices were so cheap, José knew he could sell the merchandise to stores in Laredo at wholesale and still double his
money. But he had another plan in mind. He would sell it at
retail and triple his money. For this he bought six small cases.

The next morning, Isabel prepared a big breakfast for the boys
and they drove back to Laredo without a hitch.

When José unloaded the merchandise from the car, his grandmother hit the ceiling.

"You mean you spent all your hard-earned life savings on that
stuff?" She stormed out.

The next day, when school was out, José approached the
mothers of six youngsters he had sized up as good prospects
for what he had in mind: He would take the youngsters to different parts of town and drop them off with a suitcase of merchandise to sell door-to-door for two hours after school. José would
drive around, keep an eye on them, make change, and then bring
them home. All the mothers and prospective salesmen agreed.

The plan unfolded exactly as José had envisioned it. The kids
each cleared about four dollars profit in two hours, and this José
split with them evenly. So each one made two dollars a day after school while José made as much as his whole sales force—
about twelve dollars for his two hours.

After one week, José decided to put in another four hours
on Saturday. This boosted each boy's earnings to an average of
fifteen dollars a week, more than some of their parents were
earning at full-time jobs.

At the end of the month, José took inventory so he could

reorder merchandise. Small change had been important, so he had kept the week's collection in bags. Now he emptied his four bags of change on a table and sorted it into large piles of pennies, nickels, dimes, and quarters.

"Where did you get all this money?" His grandmother had walked into the room and was now standing, arms folded on her chest, staring down at the piles of coins.

"This is what I collected in my first month of door-to-door selling," José explained, adding, "You know. The merchandise I bought in San Antonio."

She nodded and gave him a slow smile. "You know, José, this could turn out to be a pretty good little business!"

Soon José had purchased his own car, a Model A Ford coupe with a rumble seat—and plenty of storage space for merchandise.

Throughout the growth of his business life, José educated himself. It began when he asked Josefina to pass on to him the lessons she had learned in school. He was particularly interested in language—the subtle sounds of both Spanish and English words. He found that when he used the "right" words, words that triggered particular feelings in particular people, he could persuade his listeners to buy his merchandise. To learn more, he read comic books, using the pictures as an aid to visualization, and thereby inadvertently stimulating his right brain to participate.

He began to spend his spare time in the neighborhood barbershop, where there was always a stack of comic books for the waiting customers. One day, he picked up a new book he hadn't seen before. To his surprise, he could understand it.

"Can I take this home so I can finish it?" asked José.

"Wait a minute," replied the barber. "That's not a comic book you have there. It's a lesson from a correspondence course in electronics I'm taking by mail."

"I'll bring it back."

"Hey, young man, that cost me a lot of money. But I'll tell you what I'll do. I'll rent it to you for one dollar a lesson."

José thought a moment. This was 1928, when many adults were earning a wage of a dollar a day. But he was making much more.

"Agreed," he said.

"Wait," said the barber. "One more thing."

"What's that?"

"You must complete the test at the end of each lesson."

"Yes, I'll do that."

So José took the correspondence course in electronics, doing the test at the end of each lesson. When he finished the course, the *barber* received a diploma in electronics, framed it, and hung it on his wall.

For the next ten years, the diploma hung on the barber's wall, but while the barber continued to cut hair, José began to use what he had learned.

The next steps he took would change not only his life but the lives of millions of others.

Chapter 3
Putting Down Roots

As science increasingly confirms the parallels between electronic functioning and the workings of the human brain, the events that led José Silva into the electronics field take on something of the miraculous. Comic books, barbershops, electronics correspondence courses, a barber completely uninterested in the course in which he had enrolled. Was there a higher intelligence in evidence here working toward some still-undisclosed purpose?

Though the electronics bug bit José hard, there was a detour along his way toward full engagement in that direction. One day when he was fourteen, while at the barbershop, he noticed a man digging holes and spreading dirt on a vacant lot across the way. José went over to watch.

"What are you doing," he asked the man.

"I'm going to build a hamburger stand," the man replied.

"Oh, you are?" exclaimed José. "That's great."

Later, when José had finished reading comics and electronics, the man was still working to clear the land. There was an extra hoe lying by, so José picked it up and started cutting weeds.

"Wait a minute," the man called to him. "I don't want to hire you. I can't pay anybody."

"I'm not going to charge you," replied José, not missing a stroke. "I don't have anything to do right now, so I thought I'd talk with you and learn more about how you're going to build this hamburger stand."

The man agreed, and they worked and talked. His name was Mike Malus, he was Greek, and he did not speak Spanish, so the two practiced English on each other. From that afternoon on, whenever José had spare time, he would go by and pitch himself into his Greek friend's work. In the process, he learned the building business.

But for José, spare time was not all that abundant. His shoeshine/newspaper business was over now, but he ran the janitorial service at night, helped the woman collect her rents on weekends,

25

and did odd jobs in between. He was not one to lie around the house doing nothing, and he seldom participated in sports. But he did like to watch the regular Sunday baseball game when the steam laundry teams played on a vacant lot. He also enjoyed walking along the riverside to the movie theater, usually every other Sunday.

Mike finished his hamburger stand before José finished his electronics course, thanks in part to José's free assistance. Now Mike asked José to help him make hamburgers at busy times and to take his place when he had to go to the bank or handle some business. José complied—again, for free.

Soon the hamburger business was booming and the stand had developed into a full restaurant, which Malus named the Brown Derby. Now he paid José for his work in hamburgers to take home, and later he started to pay José a dollar whenever he helped out. Soon, owing to the amount of work José contributed, Mike was paying José more than he was paying his chefs.

From the enthusiasm for work José showed even before the age of six, it is clear that the boy had "hit the ground running." But in observing José's development over the decades, one begins to understand the man not as a workaholic but as a true bicameral thinker. When both their brain hemispheres are engaged, working long hours with great enthusiasm is people's normal behavior.

The Brown Derby became one of the biggest and best-known restaurants in Laredo. José's skills had him ordering supplies, preparing daily menus, and taking inventory for Mike. He even learned how to prepare meat patties, mix spices, and make fudge sauce for the sundaes. And Mike had complete trust in José. One day, when José was not yet seventeen, Mike offered him the job of restaurant manager. But José was close to completing his electronics course, and he told Mike he had a hunch that he should be going in that direction.

"Ridiculous, José. I insist you stay with me."

"I enjoy the Brown Derby. I enjoy working for you. But there's something about electronics that is pulling me," responded the boy.

"I'll double your pay."

"It's not the money, Mike. Somehow I sense there is something in this new science that is right for me."

"So be it," said Mike, extending his hand. "I wish you well."

How many young people would have had the courage to give up an enjoyable, well-paying job for a little voice that promised something new? The fear of failing at something untried is usually much louder than the call to take a chance, but not so with José. The voice that called him might have been little, but he heard it loud and clear, and he followed it.

In those days, the commercial side of the electronics field largely involved radios. These were sold by music and furniture stores. Each radio sold would require an antenna, as there were no built-in antenna radios in the early 1930s. The store would supply an antenna kit to a buyer and pay someone to install it.

José bought antenna materials in bulk—copper wire, insulators, lead-in wires, guy wires, and so on—and began producing antennas for installation on the roofs of customers' homes. He then visited all the stores in Laredo that sold radios and offered to take care of all antenna installations at a package price for materials and labor. Managers at all the stores agreed.

Once a radio was purchased, José would install the antenna on the customer's roof, connect it to the set, and adjust and tune the radio for best reception.

Remember the old song about the neck bone being connected to the backbone, the backbone connected to the hipbone . . . ? In a similar way, the hunch that led José to the inside track on Laredo's radio antenna business was connected to one electronics element after another, leading José Silva ever more deeply into the field. The antenna business led to the radio repair business. The radio repair business led to a public address system business for schools and companies. This, in turn, led to a business in repairing coin-operated phonographs both mechanically and electronically—before José combined the two approaches, the restaurants and bars that bought the machines had to call two different technicians when things went wrong.

As his expertise grew, companies were constantly offering him jobs, but these José refused. He wanted to remain independent and work for himself, contracting with others. Eventually, he structured the worldwide Silva Method operation on this same model.

When the growth of the radio business made it necessary, José bought the special tools and test equipment necessary to streamline his repair service. Since he had an established business and the vehicles necessary to do the work, his business became the biggest and best in the area.

Whenever a certain branch of his business increased, José would train others to help meet the volume of business. Where an aspect of his business decreased in profitability, for whatever reason, he would pass that business on to someone else interested in taking over, while keeping a small percentage of the profit for himself. He did this in order to concentrate his time on the more profitable activities.

Though his strategies were successful and wonderfully interesting to him, José was by no means all business. In his late teens and early twenties, he became just as interested in young women as any other youth his age. And just as any youth experiences thrills and heartbreaks, so did José. On one occasion, competition for an attractive girl led him into a fistfight. José lost both the fight and the girl. He resolved that this would never happen again.

The very next day, he joined a gymnasium and started to learn boxing. He trained for two hours a day and reached a point at which he was confident he could take on anyone, anytime. He continued to stay in condition through exercise. He was never attracted to smoking or drinking, and that helped to keep him in good physical shape.

He had one steady girl and then another, but neither arrangement ended happily. At seventeen, José was beginning to feel that perhaps he would never marry. Then his grandmother urged him to help two young visitors to Laredo enjoy their stay. They happened to be the nephew and niece of his cousin, who lived next door. Every Saturday after lunch, José, at his grandmother's urging, would take the two young visitors to the movies and show them around town. Little did he know how this would affect his life. The twelve-year-old girl soon went back to her distant home.

Eight years later, when José was nearly twenty-five, he was driving up his street when he saw his cousin accompanied by two young ladies. He turned the car around, drove back, and offered them a ride. One of the two young women was the twelve-year-old he had taken to the movies long ago.

"The girls are here on a one-month vacation," explained his cousin. "Do you think you could show them around?"

"Let's start tonight," said José, with enthusiasm. "We'll go to a dance."

Paula, the young lady, made José feel as he had never felt before in his life. "This was not just one of those girls who came across my life's path for a few dates and nothing more," he said of that first meeting. "This was a very rare, strange, unusual, and special feeling. All my thoughts about never marrying faded when I took her home that night and we were alone with each other.

"The next day was a very strange day for me. I could not think about my business, because my thoughts would come back to her again and again. I felt that I wanted to be very, very close to her.

"She was really pretty, had a lovely face. But it was not just her looks that attracted me. After all, I was twenty-five years old by this time and I had dated quite a few girls. I had some experience with the opposite sex, and that experience helped me realize that this girl was the one for me. I just knew it."

The two had a lot in common. Paula came from a small town and was devoted to her family. She had been poor like José and was not afraid to work. She went to church regularly. She was responsible, dependable, and a few years younger than he was.

Before her month's vacation was over, they had agreed that José would travel to Paula's hometown to speak to her father. "But what if he refuses me?" José wondered. He had a hunch her father would interfere.

"He won't," Paula assured him.

"Let's get married now. Then, if your father says no, we can say, 'Sorry, but we're already married.'"

"That would be an insult to my father."

Reluctantly, José agreed to the trip. And in Mexico he found

Paula's father kind and understanding, completely agreeable to all the wedding plans. The two would be married the following year.

When José returned to Laredo, he began to prepare for his marriage, looking for places to live, ordering furniture, and so forth. But suddenly he received word that Paula's father had suffered a fatal heart attack. Paula and her younger brother, Jesus, had lived alone with their father, as their mother had died when they were young. Their two older sisters were already married and had their own families.

Now an aunt of Paula's who lived in Paula's home city insisted that Paula and Jesus come to live with her. They agreed. It was now April 1940, and the wedding was to take place in a few months. José would be twenty-six in August; Paula would be twenty-one.

Suddenly, with no warning, Paula's aunt announced that there would be no wedding. Paula was too young, she asserted, and should not be permitted to marry a stranger from out of town. So José's hunch turned out to be right: Paula's father had indeed interfered with the wedding—by dying.

Both sides of the family used their influence on the aunt, but to no avail. She simply would not give in an inch. So, with everyone else in Paula's family agreeing to the marriage, it was decided that José and Paula would be married quickly—*very* quickly—by a justice of the peace at home.

Being Catholic, José had planned on a church wedding, but there seemed to be no way around the need to rush through a civil ceremony. Still, while talking over the wedding plans with Paula's family on the night before the wedding, José urged them to make one more try to persuade the stubborn aunt.

As soon as they sat down, the aunt began to blast away. "There's no sense talking about the marriage anymore. I have already made up my mind. There will not be a wedding and that is that!"

A louder voice spoke in José's mind: "This is your partner for life. Assert yourself." He arose. "Lady, forgive my bluntness. But I did not come here to ask permission to marry your niece, Paula. I came here to invite you to come to the wedding. It will take place at noon tomorrow at Paula's family home."

The blood drained from the aunt's face. She arose and pointed to the door. "You should not have come here. Leave immediately. You insult me." All rose and left, still hearing her voice calling after them, "Of course I will not come. I would not dream of coming."

It was a fine wedding—and years later even the aunt admitted to its rightness, apologizing for her behavior. But when José returned to Laredo with his bride, he had no place to take her to begin married life. His grandmother had not expected him to return as a married man. So the newlyweds lived temporarily with Paula's uncle, who also lived in Laredo.

Paula's uncle and his wife, who lived on the second floor of a building, agreed to rent the first floor to José and Paula. José divided the flat in half—one side for their home, the other for their business. And to business he returned, with enthusiasm.

José became aware that stores that sold radios accepted trade-ins. He saw huge piles of used radios stored in a warehouse.

"How much?" he asked.

"Ten dollars, if you pick. Seven-fifty, run of the mill."

"I'll take them all at five dollars apiece."

"Cash?"

"No. Ten percent down, the balance in twelve monthly payments. Interest free."

The warehouse manager scratched his head, looking around at all the space the radios were taking up.

"They're yours," he said.

José made the same deal with other radio stores. He then selected the latest models to work on first. He repaired them and painted them to look like new. Then, whenever he was called out on radio repairs, he would ask the customers if they were interested in buying a good used radio on easy terms—one dollar down and twenty cents a week. In that way, he came to sell hundreds of radios that had cost him $5 for $50, $100, and even $150. Customers paid fifty cents to a dollar a week. Now José was driving around on Sundays, not with an elderly landlady, but instead with his beautiful wife Paula. And he was not collecting money for somebody else; he was collecting his own radio money.

The kaleidoscope of business activities José had started at age six continued at twenty-six. He began to sell car radios, he converted coin-operated phonographs for use in Mexico, he sold chicks for a hatchery. And Paula helped him every step of the way.

In 1941, Dr. Ruby Lowry helped Paula deliver her first baby. José was a helper, too, though a reluctant one, since he hated to see Paula in pain. The nine-pound, ten-ounce baby boy was named José junior.

The family moved to a bigger place in January 1942. At that time, Paula was six months pregnant with her second child. This baby actually arrived ahead of Dr. Lowry. Paula delivered the child, called Isabel for José's mother, on her own.

José and Paula had an opportunity to buy the building they were living in, but someone upstaged them. Soon, though, a better house became available several blocks away. They closed the purchase of this house late in 1943, after their third child, Ricardo, was born. It was a huge, hundred-year-old house. It is still their home today, nearly half a century later.

Legend has it that the house was originally a general store. Ranchers and farmers would go there for supplies. The owners offered showers and sleeping quarters in shacks in the backyard and water troughs for the horses and mules. Today, Silva Mind Control Method lecturers come to this same house for supplies and to rest and refresh themselves.

One night, Paula was preparing dinner at about 8 P.M., when there was a knock at the door. It was one of José's customers who operated pinball machines in bars, saloons, and dance halls. Could José please go down to his bar to repair a machine, since it was a busy Saturday night? José agreed.

As José was working on the machine, a huge tough-looking character started to give him a hard time, calling him names. José recognized the 250-pound bruiser as a troublemaker who had knocked out somebody's teeth a week earlier. José tried to ignore the cursing and foul language, but finally he felt he had to take off his jacket and say, "Okay, let's go outside."

As José turned, the bully grabbed him from behind, lifted him into the air, dragged him outside, and dropped him to the ground.

José arose quickly. The man was wrapping a handkerchief around his wrist.

"I'm going to beat you up so bad," the man snarled, "even your mother won't recognize you."

The man lunged and swung. José stepped back, and the blow missed. This happened a second time. José knew then that the man was not a boxer. On the third rush, José stood his ground and counterpunched. He continued to wait until the man swung and missed. Then José swung and did not miss.

Soon the man was covered with blood, a mass of cuts and bruises. When the police arrived to break up the fight, the troublemaker pointed at José, whining, "He wanted to beat me up." The police looked at the much smaller José Silva and laughed.

One week later, José received his draft notice. He would soon be in the biggest fight the world had ever known.

At first, they drafted single young men. Then they drafted single older men. Then they drafted married men without children, next married men with one child, and after that married men with two children. Finally, they got to José, married and with three children. He passed the physical examination and was given thirty days to prepare for induction into the army. It was April 1944.

During that month, José sold all the merchandise, equipment, and vehicles he had accumulated for his business. He wanted to convert everything to cash for his wife Paula and the children, in case he did not return. Then he made plans for the family to live with his mother in San Antonio, where he was to report for basic training. This way, he would be able to see his family on weekends.

An apparently insignificant event took place during his induction process that was to change his life—and ultimately the lives of millions of people.

Recruits were given extensive interviews. The last interviewer to examine José was a psychiatrist.

"Do you wet your bed?" he asked José.

José was stunned. He had never heard of thirty-year-olds wetting their beds.

"No, sir, I do not wet my bed," he answered.

"Do you like women?" was the psychiatrist's next question. José did not know this man was a psychiatrist. In fact, he had never heard of psychiatry.

"I am thirty years old," he replied. "I'm married with three children, so you figure it out."

The psychiatrist laughed, putting José at ease. Now it was his turn to ask questions.

"What field are you in, sir, that requires the asking of such questions?"

"Psychiatry," the interviewer replied, adding, "It's medicine and psychology combined." Through further questioning, José learned that the interviewer was a lieutenant colonel and had been in psychiatry for many years.

José apologized for being so inquisitive and taking so much time while others stood waiting in line to be interviewed.

"You're not wasting time. It's all part of the interview," explained the officer. "All I want to know is whether you make sense, whether you ask questions or answer questions."

He ended the interview by giving José the name of a book he could obtain from the post library to learn more about psychiatry.

At the very next booth on the processing line, José received pamphlets and booklets about rules and regulations. All he read added up to the phrase "You're in the army now." Post services, including the chaplaincy, were described.

Included in the description was a sheet of paper with a picture of Jesus on it and a brief account entitled *One Solitary Life* by an unknown author. José gave it only a quick look. The piece was about how Jesus had lived simply and yet affected mankind mightily. Somehow, coming as it did a moment after his introduction to the study called psychology, the association stuck in José's mind. The study of psychology in association with Jesus became his life's work from that moment onward. Looking back today, José saw the double exposure as no coincidence.

Basic training was so intensive and time consuming José never had a chance to look for a book on psychiatry. It was even difficult to get a weekend pass to see Paula and the children in San Antonio. But he did get the assignment he wanted. He had requested the Signal Corps School at Camp Crowder, Missouri, lying to the interviewers in claiming he had graduated high school. They permitted him to take the electronics test, and his high score resulted in orders to proceed there after basic training.

José told Paula he would go on ahead to find a place to live near the camp. But this turned out to be impossible, and he had to settle for a furnished apartment in the city of Joplin, Missouri, about an hour's bus trip away. The rent was much higher than they could manage on his military pay and Paula's housing allotment, but they moved in anyway.

Now José faced a serious problem. He did not want to be trained as a pole climber, truck driver, or mechanic's helper. He had asked for Camp Crowder so he could train as an electronics technician. But now he discovered he needed four years of college for that training. He was called in for an interview with a lieutenant colonel, who was an administrator for the electronics department. He had lied about his high school education. Should he go that route again?

"You know, to be accepted in this department, you have to be a college graduate." The officer read the official requirements to José. "I am not in favor of your admission."

José's heart sank. High school was only a little white lie. But college?

"However . . . " The officer picked up another sheet of paper on his desk. José felt hope spring again. "In going over your records, I see that you received very high grades on your electronics tests. For this reason, I am obligated to accept you — but on one condition."

The condition was that José pass every one of the weekly Friday tests. "College graduates get a second and third chance. Not you. One failure and you are washed out and your next assignment will be pole climbing. Any questions?"

"No, sir." José knew that pole climbers had the shortest life expectancy in combat. They were picked off like birds. He rose, saluted, and left.

José passed his initial tests easily. After all, he had enjoyed fourteen years of experience with soldering irons and testing equipment. His next exams involved troubleshooting defective equipment. Here he was again on home territory, thanks to his experience in radio repair shortly after the first commercial stations went on the air. He was able to find and correct problems in ten pieces of equipment while others in the group were still wrestling with their first. Everybody watched him. Even captains.

Of course, those Friday tests were a piece of cake for him. But then came radio mathematics. He never had to know radio math when he worked with domestic equipment, but in working with government equipment it was a necessity. Pole climbing now stared him in the face. He had to learn radio math. He soon solved the problem.

Had the first sergeant inspected the barracks after official lights out, he would have discovered three college graduates learning José's time-saving tips in radio troubleshooting—in the latrines, the only place lights were left on.

"Start at the speaker end of the system and work your way back stage to stage," José told them, demonstrating by grabbing different components with his fingers. "You won't mind the shocks. They just go from finger to finger and the current is too low to hurt anybody. Listen for hums, squeaks, or thumps in the speaker. Then you know that stage is okay." He kept moving his fingers to different stages. He reached a point where there was no audible reaction in the speaker. "There! This is the dead stage."

A few minutes later, the tables would be turned. José would be the student, and the three college graduates would teach him all the math he would need to know to pass next Friday's test. And pass he did.

As the weeks of training turned into months, the high rent and high wartime prices in Joplin were beginning to hurt. Even though a regulation forbade servicemen from working in civilian jobs, José decided to go job hunting.

One evening, he walked into a shop that sold and repaired radios. The owner said, "I don't hire soldiers." The owner walked away. José had a hunch and just stood there, waiting. His intuition served him well. The owner turned and asked, "How much do you want to earn?"

José answered as he had many times before in his civilian

business life: "Whatever you think I'm worth." He had learned that people usually treated you fairly.

"Well, that's different." The owner took him down to the basement. It was piled with all types of radios that needed repair. "Go to it. I'll be back."

José worked on radios. The owner returned in two hours. "Well, how are you doing?"

"I have repaired all the radios with a red tag," José reported. "About fourteen in all."

The owner scratched his head in amazement. Then he tested each of the fourteen radios. When he found all to be in working condition, he bought José coffee next door and drove him back to the camp. He handed him ten dollars. "Okay?" he asked. "Okay," replied José.

When José had cleaned up the backlog of broken radios, his new boss agreed to allow him to work elsewhere when the going was slow. Once, when working in another shop, a fellow repairman, seeing his uniform, reminded José that a soldier cannot work in civilian jobs. José shook off the criticism and decided to work on sets that the other repairman had given up on. He fixed them all. At quitting time, the other repairman took off his civilian clothes and put on his signal corps uniform.

"We won't tell anyone, will we?" he said in a commanding voice.

"No, sir, captain," obeyed José.

José was given the rank of master sergeant and moved to South Carolina in preparation for going overseas. Paula and the children moved back to San Antonio. Shortly thereafter, José got a phone call from Paula. She told José she had to have an operation. Since she had never written about being sick, this surprised him.

"Hold off," he said to her. "I'm coming home."

He obtained a five-day leave. Traveling west, he had a gut feeling that, whatever the operation was, it was unnecessary. When he arrived in San Antonio, he learned the problem. A San Antonio doctor had examined both his wife and his sister and found them to have slight vaginal bleeding. He advised immediate hysterectomies for both. His sister acquiesced and submitted to the surgery.

"I'd better have it, too," said Paula.

"You will not be able to have any more children," José reminded her.

"We have three beautiful children—José, Isabel, and Ricardo," she reminded him.

"Let's go to Laredo and let your personal doctor decide."

Paula agreed. After Dr. Lowry examined Paula, she pronounced Paula to be in perfect health. The slight bleeding, she said, was not serious, and could be corrected with medicine.

José asked her, "Is it true what the San Antonio doctor said—that if Paula had another baby she would die?"

"Your wife can have as many children as she wants."

José looked at Paula and Paula looked at José.

The Laredo doctor was right. The couple would have seven more children: Margarita, Antonio, Ana Maria, Hilda, Laura, Delia, and Diana. Each child would remind José that education does not guarantee intelligence. The children would stimulate many feelings, hunches, and intuitions that would prove to be true over time.

The war ended before José could be shipped overseas. Instead, he was sent to Fort Bragg, North Carolina, for discharge. Paula and the children moved back to their home in Laredo and prepared to enjoy Christmas with him. However, there was a delay in the discharge process and he missed Christmas. When he arrived in Laredo, people were in the streets celebrating, fireworks were exploding, and bells were ringing. It was midnight, New Year's Eve 1946.

José brought a load of psychology books home with him. He now set himself two priorities: to read these books and reestablish his electronics business. But that was an easy work schedule for him. He felt he could do more. He happened to see an ad calling for an instructor to teach returning veterans electronics and radio repair. This sounded like a good way to make extra money until he could build up the volume of his business.

He took the Veterans Administration test and was interviewed by a Signal Corps captain.

"Your test grade was so high, the evaluators believe you cheated."

José laughed. "I know radio repair. I don't have to cheat." He related his service accomplishments and got the job at a salary commensurate with five years of teaching experience.

Some time later, when local educators started planning a junior college, they invited José to establish a radio and electronics school there. He agreed. Soon he had the Laredo Junior College electronics teaching equipment installed. On the walls of the shop were enlarged prints of circuits that student could use in learning how to troubleshoot. He also mounted dismantled electronic components on the walls. When classes began, José taught from eight in the morning until noon; after lunch, he would tend to his private electronics business.

There were two other teachers in the electronics school. They both had their own electronics businesses. One day they came to see José.

Said the first, "My business is suffering. We're teaching these vets to become our competitors."

The second agreed and proposed a solution. "José, we have to modify the curriculum. We're teaching them too much. Why should we teach them everything we know?"

José shook his head in dissent. "I feel very differently," he said. "If we treat our customers right, they'll walk right by other repair shops and come back to us."

The first teacher started to interrupt.

José went on. "Furthermore, I'm planning to hire the best students to work for me in my growing business, so I need to teach them correctly."

The two teachers left in frustration.

For the first two years of this college electronics school, the college president never bothered to come by and visit. José had a feeling there would be no academic prestige associated with this vocational facility. But then the school was inspected, rated, and awarded first place in the state of Texas. From that day on, the president visited the facility almost daily, bragging to visitors of his college's accomplishment.

By 1948, the Silvas had had three more children: twins, Margarita and Antonio, and Ana Maria. José was progressing in psychology, his business was growing, and he was becoming a skilled educator. All three ingredients seemed disconnected and unrelated, but they would coalesce into the foundation for a structure to be built later, one that would affect humanity.

However, there was still one missing ingredient.

Chapter 4
Converging Paths

In 1956, television arrived in San Antonio. Laredo was too far away to get any reception, but on weekends José took all his radio repairmen to San Antonio at his own expense to learn how to repair the early black-and-white television sets.

Then José had a hunch. He installed a television antenna atop a high tower. It worked. He had managed to capture the weak signals from San Antonio and was the first to exhibit television in Laredo. He put a television set in his shop window, and before long there was such a crowd watching that the police were called to direct traffic.

Later that year, José bought half a block of land on the highest point in Laredo. Known as Billy Goat Hill, it became the testing place for television reception. Soon José had a crew of men installing television antennas throughout Laredo while he sat in his truck studying psychology books.

What gripped his interest in particular was hypnosis, especially its early history. He learned how in the seventeenth century Athanasius Kircher experimented with cataleptic trances in animals, and how in the eighteenth century a Catholic priest named John Joseph Gassner became the first medical hypnotist. Then came Franz Anton Mesmer. The term *mesmerism* was coined for the trancelike state he induced in his patients. Mesmer's techniques were used later, in the 1800s, by Dr. James Braid, who used the word *hypnotism* to refer to the induction of trance. During Braid's time, Phineas Parkhurst Quimby and Dr. John Elliotson were using similar techniques to train clairvoyants to diagnose difficult health problems.

José was so fascinated with the idea of hypnotism that he began taking weekend classes conducted by a hypnotist in San Antonio, and by 1949, just five years after he had first begun studying psychology on his own as a soldier, he was practicing hypnosis on his children. He had formulated a procedure to help his children do better in school by toning down their hyper-

41

activity and increasing their attention spans and concentration. This he did by having them relax, both physically and mentally.

One day something happened that was to refocus all of his life experiences and his research and start him on an entirely new path. His regular practice was to read a lesson to his children while they were in a relaxed state similar to a hypnotic trance but at a level where they could still ask and answer questions. On this day, he was reading some poems to his daughter Isabel, age ten. As usual, he intended to read her the material three times, bringing her out of the relaxed level in between and then putting her back down again.

On the second reading, he put the poems in a different order. When he started to read, Isabel interrupted him and started to recite a different poem. It was the next one he had intended to read. When she finished, José began to read the next poem he had planned. Again Isabel interrupted him by reciting the one he'd planned after that. She continued to quote poems to her father, but always one poem ahead of him, as if she had known what he was going to ask her.

José was stunned. There could be no mistake about it. His daughter was reading his mind. He had seen mind-reading shows but had always discerned the trick, a code, being used. But here, in his own living room, it was really happening. He had not believed it was possible!

"Why did you quote that poem, dear. I didn't ask you to."

"I just guessed you were going to ask me."

Her answer brought Christ to his mind—he had done something like this. According to the Scriptures written some two thousand years ago, Christ had said to his disciples, "Behold, therefore, I send you prophets and wise men." Jesus, José wondered, did you mean clairvoyants?

José's procedures were successfully accomplishing the original purpose—to enable his children to improve their grades at school. Now his interest shifted from IQ to clairvoyance—he wanted to see if he could enhance his children's capacity to predict future events—through guessing.

As he read to Isabel, had his mind been broadcasting his intentions? And had his daughter's mind, when in a relaxed state, been able to function as a receiver? Did the brain have the equivalent of electronic components that were able to function as transmitters and receptors?

Isabel, with training, became even more accurate in "guessing" at what José was going to say. At first he believed she had to be in the same room with him to function in this way. But soon he hit upon the idea of having her try to diagnose illnesses, and although at first she did this in the sick person's presence, one day it became clear that she could also do it just as accurately at a distance.

A neighbor told José that her sister, who lived in Chicago, was ill with a tumor. José had Isabel enter the clairvoyant level—while she was physically and mentally relaxed—and then asked her to describe the tumor.

"It's wrapped around the heart," said Isabel. "I don't see how the doctor can get in there and remove it."

The neighbor burst into tears. "That's exactly what the doctor said," she sobbed.

José then asked Isabel to look around the Chicago house and describe what she saw.

"There's a cute red-haired baby. A woman is changing its diapers. There's a night table by the bed. It has a funny ashtray on it. I never saw an ashtray like that. It's twisted metal with the ends turned up. It's like a shell."

Some months later, the Chicago people visited Laredo. The neighbor brought them over to the Silvas' house. They scoffed at the idea that anyone could function the way Isabel had. "Hogwash!" they said.

But then Isabel described the room and the ashtray. The visitors were stunned at her accuracy. They never did believe the place hadn't been described to Isabel.

No matter. José was now convinced that through his training he had successfully turned Isabel into a clairvoyant. It was now 1953. He knew of a parapsychology laboratory at Duke University directed by a Dr. J. B. Rhine. José wrote to Dr. Rhine explaining that he had "created" a clairvoyant. Dr. Rhine responded, writing that José had probably been working with a natural clairvoyant—a person born with the gift. "We know of no reliable

source of instruction as yet on the development of psychic powers." Dr. Rhine was adamant in asserting that clairvoyance,
known as the psi factor, could not be enhanced. In this, wrote
Dr. Rhine, the psi factor was like the intelligence quotient: Some
people had more, some less. But José knew differently. He had
already enhanced the IQ factor, and now he had brought out
the psi factor.

Dr. Rhine's underlying message was that José was fooling himself. José thought not. After all, he was the subject's father, had
known her all her life, and had worked closely with her during
his research to improve her abilities in school. If she had had
any natural clairvoyant ability, as Dr. Rhine claimed, José was
sure he would have noticed.

He decided to work with others to prove to himself that his
hunch was correct—that clairvoyants *could* be trained. Over the
next ten years—1953 to 1963—he trained thirty-nine subjects indi-
vidually to function as clairvoyants. He now had a decade's worth
of carefully documented research proving he had a system for
training clairvoyants. He continued to invite Dr. Rhine to investigate the work, but the researcher never accepted the invitation.

José's method of training was rooted not in hypnosis, but in
controlled relaxation. This concept was to serve as the foundation for what would become the Silva Mind Control Method.
Whereas hypnosis involved authoritarian suggestions bordering
on commands from the practitioner, José used simple directions.
Whereas hypnosis carried relaxation to a dreamlike or trance-
like state, José kept the subject in a state of relaxation but still
in control. And whereas the hypnotic state enabled the hypnotist
to give the subject instructions that bypassed the critical faculty,
José's method enabled the subject to accept or reject instructions.

In the early 1950s, several side paths opened in José's life that
were to slow both his research and the development of his unique
training. One was José's love of singing. In an earlier year, he
had taken several months of voice lessons and had kept up his
singing as a way of relaxing from the daily routine of business.
He considered it one of two hobbies; the other was mind research.

Professional voice teachers in Laredo and San Antonio agreed
that José was good but disagreed as to whether he was a baritone

or a tenor. But on a trip to Mexico, José allowed a cousin-in-law named Joaquin to take him around to the best voice teachers in Mexico. Their decision was unanimous: José Silva was a dramatic tenor.

The last teacher to hear José sing was named Felipe, widely known as Maestro, in reference to his status as a master teacher.

"I would like to have you as a student," the Maestro told José. "Where are you from?"

"Laredo, Texas."

"Oh, you are a *gringo*."

The Maestro and the gringo made a deal. José would come to Mexico for two weeks twice a year to take two lessons a day, morning and afternoon. When he returned home, he would carry with him a program of practice prepared by the Maestro.

In 1956, on the final day of the second two-week intensive, José found about fifty students waiting at the Maestro's home. But when he walked through the door, the Maestro called to him. "*Gringo*, you are next." José assumed the students were there for some other event and that the Maestro just wanted to get him out of the way.

The Maestro led José through several arias from such operas as *Aïda*, *Tosca*, and *Paggliacci*. The final aria was "Che-Gelida Manina" from *La Bohéme*. This was a challenge to José, as it was written for a lyric tenor. When he finished, the Maestro turned his chair around to face José.

"*Gringo*, we can teach you no more in Mexico. To complete your training to sing complete operas, you should go to where this can be done best—Italy. I am authorized by the Mexican government to present you with a scholarship."

"But, Maestro," replied José, "I am a United States citizen—a *gringo*."

"Your father was a Mexican citizen. That is enough. I am offering you a two-year scholarship to go to Milan to complete your voice training."

"I am forty-two years old. Isn't that too old?"

"You will still have fifteen to twenty years of singing."

Now José realized why all of the students were there. He was handed the award and they all applauded.

José was flattered by the award, and ever afterwards treasured the memory of that day. But it was his hobby, mind control, that drew him. Nevertheless, though he eventually turned down the scholarship, like everything else that happened in his life, singing would have its part to play in what was to come. At present José lectures all over the world, sometimes eight hours a day, for as many as ten days straight, and he is thankful indeed for the voice training.

If singing represented one detour that ultimately led back to his interest in the mind, his thriving business continued to represent another. In business, José had always had the "luck" to come up with the right idea at the right time. As a young boy, he got the idea of taking lemon juice, mixing it with sugar, and letting the mixture dry into a powder. He packaged the powder and went door to door selling this instant lemonade during the hot summer months, years before any commercial products of this sort became available.

In 1951, he saw the need for special equipment when a second television station began operating near Laredo. The first station had been established in San Antonio, 150 miles to the north. Now a second, on the very same channel 4, was installed in the Rio Grande Valley, about 150 miles southeast. This caused reception problems in Laredo. Viewers would get two pictures superimposed over each other, or sometimes they would get the picture from one station and the sound from the other.

Television dealers began complaining to the manufacturers, because customers began coming in to return their sets. Three major factories sent engineers to survey the problem. All reported back that Laredo was well beyond the fringe reception area and should not be receiving any signal. Furthermore, since both stations were on the same channel, there was no way to "wave trap" one without "wave trapping" both, meaning that both were received.

The same problem was affecting Corpus Christi, 135 miles due east of Laredo. A lot of television sets were involved. José decided to run some experiments.

The shape of television antennas make them largely directional. You must aim an antenna properly to get the best reception.

But some unwanted signal is picked up from the rear. Usually this "front-to-back" ratio is strong enough to drown out the unwanted signal, but not in Laredo. José devised a small antenna to be installed on the same mast with the main antenna but facing the unwanted direction. The signal from this small antenna was fed into the main antenna but 180 degrees out of phase so that it cancelled out the unwanted signal in the main antenna.

At around the time that José was tackling this problem, the Laredo Air Base was selling some barracks. José bought one, cut it in half, and installed the halves side by side on his property to give him more space for his electronics business. Later, one of these structures was covered with brick and became the administration building for Silva Mind Control International, Inc.

José's new antenna became an overnight success. The word reached Corpus Christi, where a large distributor offered to pay the expenses of television service people in the area if José put on a demonstration. José agreed.

He set up two installations, one with the old standard antenna and one with his new antenna. He also set up two television sets as demonstrators. When the invited guests arrived, he had both sets switched to the old equipment. The pictures were all messed up and rolling.

"Hey, no difference at all!" "You're wasting our time." "You brought us all the way here to see that?"

José got what he wanted: everybody's attention.

"Now," he said, "watch the picture as I turn on our channel separator for this set." He activated the switch and a clear picture popped into view. The other set was still in turmoil.

The technicians were astonished. Their factory engineers had told them it couldn't be done.

"Now, I'm going to switch from San Antonio to the valley television station," José announced. When he turned the switch, the picture changed and the valley station came in sharp and clear.

The technicians asked to see what was inside the box. José had already applied for the patent rights, but he had played it safe by having the mechanism box soldered closed.

"Opening the box is against company policy," José explained.

He then announced that the company was selling not the box itself, but a package: a TV set and antenna, tuned, aligned, and fully functioning.

José sold many complete installations and made good money on that idea. He continued to profit from it until a television station was built in Laredo and the channel separation equipment was no longer needed.

Eventually, José came to own a number of patents involving electronics that would be in use and bring him income for prolonged periods. But when an electronics activity threatened José's attention to mind research, it seemed to drop out of the picture.

One such idea had to do with phonographs.

In the 1950s, coin-operated phonographs were being installed in restaurants, bars, and dance halls on a commission basis by route operators who shared the take equally with the owners. But these route operators would not permit the phonographs to be repaired, so when one broke down, the owner had to buy a new one from the route operator.

José found that the route operators would trade the broken machines for new ones from the distributors. The distributors would then fill a freight car with these used machines and sell them outside the country, usually in Mexico.

With financial backing, José bought the used trade-ins from the distributors, repaired them, replaced all the worn-out parts, painted the cabinets, and sold them to the same restaurants, bars, and dance halls for three times what they cost him. The price was still less than that for a new phonograph, but more important, José offered his buyers a service agreement that considerably extended the life of the phonograph.

Soon his converted barracks were ringing with the sound of old phonographs arriving, being repaired, and leaving in a refurbished condition. To keep up with repairs, José had to install three phonograph service stations seventy-five miles apart. After a year and a half, he had sold two million dollars' worth of reconditioned phonographs, and his cost had been only one-third that amount. José felt that he had found his life's work.

"Oh, really?" asked a higher intelligence. It had other plans for him.

Chapter 5
Research Takes Over

Hypnosis continued to fascinate José. In its study and human practice, he saw the greatest promise for understanding the mind. During the 1950s, he spent many a weekend in a nearby city taking courses in hypnosis. He gathered as many books as he could on the subject—by Mesmer, Braid, Russo, LeCron, and Erickson—and studied them deeply.

One day, Paula came running into his office from their house next door. "Come home quick, José. See what Isabel is doing!" There was fright in her voice.

José ran with her back to the house. There he saw Ricardo, seven, walking slowly down the hall, his arms extended as though walking in his sleep.

"A little to the right. Now to the left." Isabel was directing her brother, step by step. She had obviously hypnotized him. This had taken place in the bedroom and now she was directing him to a chair in the living room.

"Stop them! Stop them!" cried Paula.

"Sh-h-h," motioned José. "I want to watch this."

Paula threw her hands up in exasperation.

When Ricardo was seated, Isabel gave him a posthypnotic suggestion. "Every time I snap my fingers, you will yell as loud as you can 'Rah, rah, rah, Isabel!' three times." Isabel then brought Ricardo out of the hypnotic state. He looked around and was surprised to see his parents standing by. Isabel snapped her fingers. Ricardo's booming voice made the windows rattle.

"Rah, rah, rah, Isabel! Rah, rah, rah, Isabel! Rah, rah, rah, Isabel!"

Isabel then told Ricardo he would forget everything that had happened.

By this time, Paula was outraged at José. "Why didn't you stop them?"

"I didn't know she had been reading my books on hypnosis. I wanted to see how well she had learned her lessons." Then,

turning to Isabel, he said, "Darling, you did not have to bring
Ricardo down the hall step by step. You could have given him
a posthypnotic suggestion in the bedroom that when he opened
his eyes he would walk into the living room, sit in a certain chair,
close his eyes, and enter the hypnotic state again."

Isabel nodded knowingly.

"Don't encourage her, José," admonished Paula. "She shouldn't
practice hypnosis on other children."

José shrugged off the criticism, but soon realized that his wife
had been talking good sense. One day he found a group of his
workers looking out the window and chuckling. Isabel was with
them. José went outside to see what it was all about.

A policeman whom José knew well was parked out in front.
Ricardo was leaning against the police car talking to the policeman. "I just robbed a bank. Take me to jail."

"You did not rob a bank, Ricardo," the policeman replied. "Stop
kidding."

This was repeated several times. José could tell that Ricardo
had been hypnotized. He smiled at the policeman and motioned
him to wait. José went inside, gave Isabel instructions, and she
came out to the police car. Isabel apologized to the policeman
and brought Ricardo back into the house. There, under José's
instructions, she told him that he did not rob a bank, that she
was just playing, and that he would remember the whole ordeal.
Then she brought him out.

"You should never let your hypnotized subject get so far away
from you, Isabel," cautioned José. "What if a passing car had
had a blowout? It would have shocked Ricardo into awakening.
He then might have started running, perhaps into an oncom-
ing car."

José then stepped out of the role of teacher and into that of
father. "Hypnosis is nothing to play with. You will not use it
again unless I am present." Paula, he saw, had been right.

Still, though he castigated Isabel, he did not want to discourage
her altogether from her interest in hypnotism. His fatherly command was delivered in the form of a verbal slap on the wrist.
Oddly, it would not be long before José himself would receive
a more serious reprimand.

Over the years, José had continued to research hypnosis with his children, putting particular effort into preconditioning them for potential emergencies. One evening, the Silvas had friends over for dinner. Included was a doctor, also interested in hypnosis, and the doctor's wife. José was serving drinks before dinner—he himself did not partake of alcoholic beverages until years later, when he was sixty—and one extra drink had been left on a side table. Margarita, then fifteen, drank it down and became quite intoxicated.

Paula put Margarita to bed, but the girl kept moving from side to side and uncovering herself. The doctor advised that she be well covered to keep her body temperature from dropping too much and too quickly from the chemical shock. The doctor kept checking her temperature with a thermometer under her armpit.

"I don't like what's happening," he said.

"Let me tell you something," interjected José, "All my children, including Margarita, have been preconditioned for emergencies through hypnosis. They know that should they ever need help, all I need to do is place my thumb on their foreheads, count from ten to one, and they will be at a deep state of mind where pain and other conditions can more easily be corrected."

"Try anything." There was urgency in the doctor's voice. "Margarita's body temperature is dropping fast and it has me worried."

José moved to the bed. He put the thumb of his right hand on her forehead and with his left hand held her head to keep it from moving. Slowly he started to count, "Ten, relax, nine, relax, eight, relax, . . . " and so on. When he reached the count of one, Margarita stopped moving and appeared to be in a deep sleep.

Keeping his thumb on her forehead, José said to her, "You are going to sleep for two hours. You will then wake up refreshed. You will have no discomfort in your body, no headache, no buzzing in your ears. You will feel fine and in perfect health. You will be hungry and want something to eat." He removed his thumb. The doctor took her temperature.

"It's stabilized."

A few minutes later, he took it again. "It's starting to go back up." He removed some of the blankets. After a few moments and another temperature measurement, the doctor announced, "Margarita's temperature is back to normal. Take off all the blankets."

While back in the dining area having dinner, the doctor confessed he had never seen a person's body temperature come back to normal as fast as Margarita's had done. After dinner, he stayed where he was. "I want to see what happens to Margarita at the end of two hours."

On the dot of two hours, Margarita came walking down the hallway. She stretched and said, "What is there to eat? I'm hungry."

The doctor shook his head in disbelief. "Now I've seen everything."

Not quite *everything*.

He had not seen José Silva do age regression.

When a subject is hypnotized and directed to go back in time, the subject obeys and is able to describe places visited and events experienced even in infancy. If regressed further in time, the subject may begin to talk in a different language or dialect, or may describe events in another lifetime. Some twenty-five years ago, this author collaborated with a hypnotist on a book entitled *What Modern Hypnotism Can Do for You.** In it, the hypnotist describes a case of unintentional reincarnation. His hypnotized client, a teacher who was having trouble with her memory, suddenly began talking in Old English and describing her unhappy life as a waif who had been raped and beaten and had run away from home. The hypnotist ended the session and invited a historian to attend the next one. Everything checked out. Yes, you could cross the River Avon on foot that year due to a drought. Yes, a village by that name existed there. Yes, there was such a cult in those days.

In the mid-1950s, José went through literally hundreds of sessions of age regression, each adding credibility to the idea of reincarnation. One nine-year-old girl named Mary was extremely detailed in her descriptions of her past life. When José took Mary

*New York: Hawthorn Publishing Company, 1965.

back before birth, she told him she was twenty-three years old and living in Paris. She understood French and knew the Paris sights. Since José had not been to Paris and could not confirm what she told him, he sought out a brother at St. Joseph's Academy who had lived in Paris for a while. With the brother when José visited was the editor of the *Laredo Times*. The brother agreed to see the girl, and the editor, who knew of José's research, asked to come along.

After inducing age regression in the little girl, José introduced her to the brother, who questioned her thoroughly. Mary mentioned a big church.

"Do you know the name of the big church?" the brother asked her.

"You mean Notre Dame?"

The brother motioned to José and the editor that the girl was right.

"In what direction does the river flow—toward the back or front of the church?"

Again the answer was correct.

"If you enter the church at the front, what is on your right?"

The girl answered as if she were there.

"Where is the opera house in relation to the museum?"

Another right answer.

José then progressed Mary to the point in that life at which she married. She described the church, the wedding, her wealthy husband, and the excellent cook who prepared the meal.

"Call the cook; I want to talk to him," said José.

José watched as the little girl, who, in this life, had never been to Paris, turned her head as if talking to somebody.

"He'll be here in a minute," she said.

They continued talking about other things until the little girl said, "The cook is here. What do you want to know?"

"Ask your cook to give us the name of a popular recipe in France," said José.

There was a brief wait, then "*Pato a la Deutsch*," she announced.

"Would he be so kind as to give us the recipe so we could prepare it?"

"Get paper and pencil," Mary ordered.

José and the brother wrote down the ingredients and the preparation steps as the *Laredo Times* editor watched. Occasionally, the brother would ask a question in French and she would reply correctly in English.

When the session was over, the three men went looking for a French chef. They found one in a Laredo hotel's restaurant.

They told the chef that they were gourmets, always looking for exotic recipes to prepare themselves.

"I came across a dish called *Pato a la Deutsch*. Do you know such a dish?"

"*Oui, monsieur. C'est formidable!*"

The brother interpreted. "He says there is and it's good."

The chef was asked to write down the ingredients. When the three returned to José's office, they compared the chef's recipe with the little girl's version. They were exactly alike. The only difference was a cosmetic one—the regression chef preferred to use fruit balls instead of cubed fruit.

The *Laredo Times* editor was so impressed with what he had seen that he wrote an article recounting the session and suggesting that the experiment made a good case for reincarnation.

Ninety percent of Laredo's population is Catholic. Ever since the Council of Nicea some fifteen hundred years ago, when all references to reincarnation were removed from the literature, reincarnation has been a taboo subject for Catholics. So when this article appeared in the *Laredo Times*, many readers complained to the managing editor. He was not a Catholic, but he was a follower of Christian Science, a faith that considers hypnosis to be the work of the devil. This managing editor demoted the editor to reporter and swore to José that the newspaper would never again publish anything about his mind research.

The manager lived up to his word. He kept all mention of the Silva work out of the newspapers for more than ten years, until he retired. By that time, José had completed his research, fine-tuned the training, and launched the Silva Mind Control Method. It made quite an impact on the national press, but José remained unknown in his own hometown.

After the old managing editor retired, in the early 1970s, José decided to address the local news boycott against him. One day, he went down to the *Laredo Times* to see the new managing editor. He brought with him a large box. After they had shaken hands, José opened the box and extracted dozens of articles published about him and his method in major newspapers and magazines all over the United States. He then proceeded to spread them out on the floor of the manager's office.

"What on earth are you doing?" cried the surprised managing editor.

José started to call out the cities as he pointed to the clippings now covering every inch of floor space. "Chicago, New York, Boston, Houston." Then he looked the editor in the eye. "It makes no sense that every paper has published articles about our work except our hometown newspaper. No sense at all." He slapped the manager's desk for emphasis.

"José Silva," protested the manager, "that's all going to change now. From now on things will be different."

Within a week, a full-page story appeared in the *Times* on the Silva Method and its rapid growth and acceptance. From that day on, José got his share of local publicity. Now there are two daily newspapers in Laredo, both willing to air what they don't always pretend to understand—the man with the mind control method that swept the world.

Throughout the years in which José's method was taking shape, his regression work continued to be a mainstay. José spent ten years—1953 through 1963—on regression and progression work, mostly the former, and during this period he trained thirty-nine clairvoyants, all volunteers from his family and circle of friends. To study the extraordinary faculties of the human mind, he conducted literally hundreds of age-regression sessions.

It is interesting to note that the training of these thirty-nine clairvoyants bore little resemblance to the training of the ten million clairvoyants by what later came to be known as the Silva Method.

The thirty-nine were trained purely by going through scores and scores of regression sessions. They were hypnotized and taken back in time. Regression became José's doorway to the human mind. This was the beginning but hardly the end. He was to discover as he stood in that doorway that the mind had secrets to reveal, secrets that science has not been able to fully explain to this day.

José found that relaxation was the first step, not only for the thirty-nine clairvoyants but also, later, for the ten million Silva Method trainees.

Scientists later confirmed that relaxation slowed brain-wave frequency. They called the relaxed mental state alpha. The brain encephalogram measured these brain-wave frequencies. José found that information could be fed into the mind at the alpha level and memory enhanced. Scientists later confirmed the computerlike, or cybernetic, aspects of the human brain. José found that subjective thinking during meditation was a valuable adjunct to problem solving. Scientists later confirmed that subjective thinking was right-brain thinking and that two hemispheres were better than one.

But we are getting ahead of our story.

José's sessions with the thirty-nine clairvoyants gave him an opportunity to try different induction techniques — for example, authoritarian, permissive, passive, and dynamic.

When this period ended and José decided to move on to other mind research, he had reached one conclusion — or rather semiconclusion, as he called it, giving himself the latitude to change it if he came across conflicting evidence. The semiconclusion was this: After a number of hours of regression, subjects appeared to be more intuitive than beforehand. For some, this intuitive faculty would appear when least expected, and it would also disappear suddenly. It seemed to José that a subject had to be at a particular mental level to be able to function in a highly intuitive way.

This led José to develop a regression-induction system that would enable a subject to stay at the level of optimum intuitiveness. Inducing regression in this way was *not* hypnosis. In fact, over the ten-year period he spent studying regression, José found that hypnosis worked against his purposes.

For one thing, the mind of a hypnotized subject functioned *inductively,* and not deductively. And people in hypnosis do not ask questions; they only answer them. Both deductive powers and inquisitiveness, José learned, are necessary to the expansion of the mental powers.

Next, the deeper hypnotic subjects go, the more easily they forget what took place there. But José wanted his trainees to remember more at *whatever* mental level they were. And finally, a person acting under a posthypnotic suggestion functions primarily at twenty cycles per second, which is beta, the level that is associated with the objective, physical senses and left-brain dominance. José discerned that his subjects had to function at ten cycles per second, the alpha level, which is associated with the subjective senses and, as science later discovered, where right-brain functioning is on par with the left.

To sum up José's years of research: 1944–1949—the study of psychology and the brain; 1949–1952—applying mind training techniques to help children to do better in school; 1953–1963—training thirty-nine clairvoyants by teaching them to use their alpha brain level and, though he did not realize it, their right-brain hemisphere.

The research, then, underwent a transformation over its two decades. José went from burning the midnight oil with an insatiable appetite for knowledge about the human brain to utilizing that knowledge for the benefit of his own children's mental acuity and to encouraging the human mind to divulge its secrets.

Let's examine this latter activity. There were no cadavers lying in a sanitary white laboratory with their heads cut open and high-powered microscopes aimed at their gray matter. There were no chemicals, burners, or panels of blinking lights.

There was merely a man in a living room with some family and friends, a man interested in the subject of the human mind, especially its ability to transcend space and time. If any laboratory protocol was involved, it was written in the creative realm from whence it seeped into José's brain in the form of intuition—to do this with one person and to try that with another person.

Just as more formal laboratory procedures would involve trial and error, so did these living room procedures lead to failure more often than success. But gradually the successes that did occur began to add up to a way to harness these secrets of the human mind, unleash them, and produce superminds: the foundation for the Silva Method.

After working with the thirty-nine clairvoyants, José's next step was to assemble groups to work with in order to turn out greater numbers of superminds. At the same time, José needed to refine the procedures to determine how much time and training were needed for such groups to function clairvoyantly.

José invited his neighbors to permit their children to benefit from his research. Until then, the neighbors had looked with a leery eye at what was going on behind the Silva walls. "Of the devil!" they said. "Weird." "Crazy." "Dangerous!" These words were all used out of ignorance. José wanted to change all that by throwing open the doors to his home.

At first, certain neighbors would bring their kids to observe as José worked with others.

"Don't touch my kids!" they warned.

But José's trainees not only did better at school, they improved their personalities, home relationships, and moods. The hesitant neighbors became convinced of the benefits.

Their song changed. It became, "When are you going to work with my child?" "Don't leave my child for the last!"

Chapter 6
A Healer Is Born

In the late 1950s and early 1960s, José Silva's research began to focus more and more heavily on using the mind for better health. In this effort, he was both student and teacher, attempting to develop ways to heal others himself. There were no volunteer students for this phase as in the clairvoyant training. José offered to heal whenever the opportunity presented itself, even if this meant taking time off from his electronics business. In fact, the emphasis of that business was more and more on the electronic monitoring of human brain waves and their physiological effects, as the biofeedback equipment industry began to emerge.

As a developing healer, José had already acquired tools from his work with hypnosis. He knew the importance of expectation, belief, and suggestion. He knew that these conditions produced the placebo effect. And he had clues that the imaging power of his own mind could assist the healing power of the patient's mind. He worked on this assumption some thirty years ahead of the first outside clinical demonstrations of the amazing powers of the mind.

José used each request for healing help as a means to perfect his personal methodologies. He developed several healing approaches, each of which seemed to work under its own special conditions. Eventually, he merged these into a three-cycle method. If the first cycle did not produce a healing, he would go through the second cycle, and then, if he had to, the third.

In the first cycle, José would go to bed, relax, visualize the sick person's face, and work at recalling the sound of the voice and, where the two had shaken hands, the feel of the hand. Then he would hold his breath and imagine the sick person getting well. He reasoned that by holding his breath until he was short of oxygen, he would be creating a state of emergency within his mind and body, and that this would result in more mental energy and thus a more effective contact. He asked the patient to participate, not by being physically present with him, but by drinking half a glass of water just before going to bed and finishing it on arising. José would practice this method for three nights, each time assuming that the cause of the problem was psychologically based even though it appeared to be organic. If after the three nights there was no improvement, José went on to the second healing cycle.

The second cycle was identical to the first, except that this time José proceeded on the assumption that the disease or physical problem was purely organic in nature. Again, after three nights, if the problem remained uncorrected, José administered the third cycle. Now he approached the problem as one that was neither psychological nor organic, but that had been given to the patient by a parent or had come to the patient from somewhere else at birth.

In one of his first tests, when asked to help a six-month-old baby who had had a serious allergy since birth, José went the whole three cycles. Three days after he completed the third cycle, the allergy disappeared.

The three-cycle method evolved further as José saw new and different ways to use the mind as a helping tool. One day, when he phoned for an appointment to see a Catholic priest who lived two blocks away from his home, he was told that the priest had a problem with his knee and would be spending the day in bed. José decided to help.

"I know he's been plagued with this problem for some fifteen years," explained José. "That's exactly why I wish to see him."

He got the appointment.

"What can I do for you?" asked the priest when José entered. He was sitting in a rocking chair.

"On the contrary," replied José. "It is I who want to help you. And I think I can help with that knee problem."

"Are you a doctor?"

"No, but I am researching a new science. I sincerely believe it can help in your case."

"What is the name of this new science?"

"It does not have a name yet, but it comes under the heading of parapsychology."

"Let me think about it. I'll let you know."

A month later, the priest called to ask José to come over.

"Listen to this strange coincidence," said the priest. "Two days after you left, I received a pamphlet in the mail advertising a new book. It listed a chapter on parapsychology. I sent for it and read it. The book was *Experimental Psychology* by Siwek. You may start anytime you wish."

José was pleased that the priest had used the word *coincidence*. He understood the word to mean a spontaneous happening whose end results are constructive, as opposed to destructive, as the word *accident* implies. He recalled another instance in which the word coincidence had come up and caught his attention not too long before.

A few years back, José had closed his business at 9 P.M., as was his custom. He had dinner, helped Paula put the children to bed, and then settled down to his usual several hours of study. While reading a difficult section in a psychology text, he suddenly had a sense of the futility of it all. He had a busy schedule planned for the next day at the office, and there he was wasting good hours of sleep studying something that, if the truth be told, wasn't even making sense to him. He slammed the book closed, threw it on the floor, and watched it slide under a couch.

Paula heard the noise and came in to see if the book had fallen from his hands as he fell asleep, a common occurrence. But she saw that he had thrown it down on purpose. José did go to sleep right after that, but about two hours later he suddenly awoke. A bright light, like a midnight sun, filled the inside of his head. And hanging in space he saw two sets of numbers: 3-4-3 and, below this, 3-7-3. Then came an impression of Christ and the tract called *One Solitary Life* that had been given to him at the army reception center.

"Why Christ?" he asked himself in wonder. "Why me? Why the numbers?"

He opened his eyes. It was dark. The clock on the table read 4:30.

Maybe this was a message, he thought. He closed his eyes. The light inside his head was still there, but fading. He tried to keep it from disappearing by changing position and breathing slowly, but the light continued to fade, and soon it was gone. José lay awake trying to analyze what had happened.

He recalled one of Paula's favorite warnings to him: "They say that people who read too much go crazy!" He certainly would not tell her about the light in his head. The impression of Christ and the *One Solitary Life* seemed to confirm that the experience was authentic and positive.

In the morning, José's first priority was to track down any significance the two sets of numbers might have. On a vague hunch, he went through the entire Laredo phone book, but saw no such listing. His next impulse was to go to someone whose address contained the numbers. Maybe such a person had a message for him. But there were no such addresses on the city map. By midafternoon, José was watching automobile and truck license plates as they drove by. None matched.

At 8:45 P.M., José was starting to close his business, when Paula came in from their house next door. "José," she said, "if you go across the river into Nuevo Laredo for a service call this evening, would you bring me a bottle of alcohol?"

Because Mexican alcohol was pure, it could be used for medicinal purposes. Mexican merchants put cubes of camphor in bottles of alcohol when they sell it to Americans. When the tax people at the border smell the camphor, they don't charge a tax.

"I don't have any service calls from across the border, honey," José replied, "but I will go and get you a bottle anyway."

At that very moment, in walked an old friend of José's.

"Want to join me for coffee?" he asked José.

"Help me close my place and we'll go right now," replied José. As they were closing windows and turning off lights, José asked him, "You in a hurry?"

"No. Got all the time in the world. Why?"

"I want to go across the river and get my wife a bottle of alcohol."

"Sure. I'll go with you."

While driving to the bridge, José felt he could confide in his friend about what happened to him in the night. Since he, too, had studied psychology, he was not likely to call José crazy. So José told him all the details of that night's happening. Suddenly, while they were driving across the bridge into Mexico, his friend blurted out, "Hey, perhaps there's such a number in Mexico's lottery!"

While José was buying the alcohol with camphor, his friend strolled into an adjoining room of the liquor store. José heard him call, "What numbers are you looking for?"

"3-4-3 and 3-7-3."

"3-4-3 is here."

José did not believe him. "You're kidding."

"Come and see for yourself."

Sure enough, hanging on a display string were five segments of an active series numbered 3-4-3. There were five units left of the original twenty units. José bought all five. And later the number won! After paying the Mexican income tax and converting the money into United States dollars, José cleared ten thousand dollars, in those days worth several times what it's worth today. Still, later he learned that the other series, 3-7-3, had been on sale only in Mexico City. His winning 3-4-3 was on sale only in Nuevo Laredo.

In his mind, José went over the sequences of events that had led to the buying of those tickets. Two hours after he had decided to discontinue the study of psychology and tossed the book on the floor, he had seen the light, Christ, *One Solitary Life*. Then came his wife's request, his reply—which could have been quite different—and his friend's arrival. What timing! A chain of a dozen "coincidences." Needless to say, José searched out the book that had slid under the couch that night. He pulled it out, dusted it off, and went back to his studies.

Years later, a similar set of circumstances had taken him to the bedside of the priest, who himself had called José to him as a result of "coincidence." José figured that arrival of the pamphlet the priest had received had indeed been a coincidence, since it must already have been in the mail when José first visited him. Another coincidence, which gave the priest easy access to the book announced in the pamphlet, was that the book's author was a professor at a Catholic university. The book had three official Catholic permissions, all crediting the book's value for the priest.

José moved his chair closer to the priest's bed.

"I will talk. You listen. If you have a question, please hold it until later."

The priest nodded his agreement.

José began to talk. He talked about the weather, Laredo's business climate, international affairs, his own family and business. He talked for an hour about everything except the priest's knee problem. His purpose was to create in the priest's mind a state of monotony, then fatigue, then confusion. Each time José detected this state of confusion, he did his own mental picturing, because the confused mind is more receptive to the programming effects of imagery.

Three times during his one-sided conversation, José detected this state in the priest and began his mental picturing. First, he visualized the priest standing in front of him with the knee problem. Then he pictured a second scene to the left of the first: the priest drinking half a glass of water at night and the other half in the morning and the problem disappearing. Finally, in a third mental picture, again slightly to the left, José imagined the priest walking in perfect health and able to kneel in prayer.

José got up from his chair. "Father, there is only one thing you need to do to contribute to your healing. Before retiring, get a glass and fill it with water. Then drink half the water and the other half first thing in the morning."

"When are you going to start the healing?" asked the priest.

"I've already started," he announced.

The priest's shoulders sagged in disappointment. There was more disappointment in his voice. "Is this how you heal? Talk, talk, and more talk?"

"Yes, Father. I'll be back in three days to check on our progress."

When José returned in three days, the priest was standing tall and erect. His face brightened when he saw José.

"I haven't felt this well in fifteen years. It's a miracle!"

"No, Father, it's a coincidence." José believed that help had come from some higher dimension of intelligence.

They sat down to discuss the healing.

"I'm a sinner," said José. "You're an angel. How can a sinner help an angel who has been suffering for fifteen years?"

"One has to suffer in order to merit," replied the priest.

"But not knowing how to solve the problem lengthens the time of suffering. So ignorance does not exempt us from suffering," offered José. "We suffer from not knowing any better."

The experience caused the priest to become a strong supporter of José's work—work devoted, as José had put it, to knowing better. This was support José clearly needed as his reputation as a healer grew. As he experimented with different approaches, he developed techniques to match specific problems. His many interesting cases brought him more and more challenges and resulted in a wide array of "customized" healings.

For example, a Laredo rancher suffered from migraine headaches every time he ate a dairy product. The headaches would disable him for two or three days. José explained his research, and the man agreed to spend a day with him. José worked on the man as he had done with the priest. First he confused him. Then he mentally pictured three scenes: first, the problem; next, the man eating butter and enjoying it; and third, the man able to enjoy dairy products headache free.

At lunch that day, the two went to a restaurant. José ordered bread with double servings of butter.

"Have some bread and butter," invited José.

"I love butter. But it poisons my system."

"It *used* to poison your system, but it doesn't anymore," José responded. José pushed his own portion in front of him.

"Are you crazy? Do you want me to suffer for days?"

"You *used* to suffer, but not anymore. Eat the butter, my friend."

"I thought you were joking. Well, just remember it will be you who has ruined my week."

"I was *going* to ruin your week, but not anymore," countered José.

The rancher started to spread the butter on a slice of bread.

"Wait," said José. "Put twice as much on."

"You really want to knock me out, don't you?"

"This stuff *used* to knock you out, but no more," responded José.

After the rancher ate two slices with a thick layer of butter, José asked him, "How long did it usually take for the effect to come on?"

"Fifteen minutes" was the answer. When that time passed and the man had experienced no ill effects, he said, "Sometimes it takes twenty minutes."

"Not anymore," José reminded him. A few minutes later, "You are overdue."

"Sometimes it takes longer."

"It *used* to take longer, but not anymore."

The rancher never did get a headache, and was able to enjoy dairy products thereafter.

In another dramatic example, José was contacted by one of the daughters of a woman who had lost so much weight her family was expecting her to die. Two daughters carried their mother in and explained that it had all started after the woman had eaten oysters one night for dinner. Since then, she had had epileptic seizures every few minutes around the clock. Then a third elder daughter arrived.

"No one is going to experiment with my mother. There are too many frauds." Before she could go on, her mother had a seizure. The daughters applied alcohol to the back of her head.

When things had settled down, José asked the skeptical daughter, "How could I be dealing fraudulently when I do not charge for my services?"

She softened a bit, and José explained that all her mother would have to do was drink one half glass of water on retiring and one on rising. When the young woman raised no objection, he began his three-part visualization.

Three days later, the woman had not suffered a single seizure and had even enjoyed oysters for dinner.

One young man who had just been wed was unable to consummate his marriage owing to impotency. He was despondent and suicidal when he went to José. In one month he reported a slight improvement. José continued to do his mental work. By the end of the second month, the couple were beginning to have normal relations. By the end of the third month, they were enjoying a happy marital life.

One man was so cancer infested that he had to be kept unconscious with drugs. As soon as consciousness returned, he started to scream with pain. José had to work on him while he was in a comatose state. Doctors watched his every step, but were called to other cases when José started his conversation. He reminded the anesthetized man of the many reasons he had for getting well: so he could get married, have a family, be a good citizen, help God to solve the planet's problems, and so on. Every day, José went to the hospital and worked the three-cycle routine for an hour.

At the end of the third day, the mother reported that her son was staying awake for short periods without pain. Then, in the next forty-five days, he gained nineteen pounds and needed only one injection of Demerol a day. The doctors were amazed. They had predicted a quick demise. The man was taken to Houston for a thorough examination, and the final report declared the patient to be completely free of cancer.

One of José's former partners heard about this particular case and asked, "How much did you get paid?"

"I do not charge a fee," José responded.

"How about the bridge toll, your gasoline, the valuable time you lose from your business?" He then figured it out. "You put in forty-five hours plus cash expenses."

"But I reaped the experience," replied José. His friend was not impressed.

That night, José and Paula went to a church bingo night, and José won the prize: five hundred dollars. His friend was at the bank the next morning when José went to deposit the money. He showed the friend the check. "See?" he said. "Ten dollars an hour for the forty-five hours and fifty dollars for bridge toll."

One night, José agreed to speak to some doctors at the hospital about his method. They were so intrigued that they took him to an even larger meeting. Here the interest centered on the medical applications of hypnosis. They asked question after question and then called for a demonstration. By this time, it was past midnight. José suggested a new date be set when there would be more time.

Two weeks later, on a Sunday afternoon, accompanied by two

of his sons and two of his daughters, José arrived at the meeting. More than fifty physicians were in attendance, some from as far away as 150 miles away.

A doctor who served as spokesman explained that José Silva had kindly accepted their request to demonstrate some uses of hypnosis as it applied to medical practice. When he stepped up to the stage, José received polite applause.

"I'm going to select one of you as a subject." He pointed to a young man, a "Dr. R." The man joined José on stage.

"Please sit in this chair, Dr. R."

Using a standard induction technique, José hypnotized Dr. R. He then explained to the audience that he would cause the effects of flaccid paralysis on Dr. R.'s left arm. José then touched Dr. R.'s left arm with the index fingers of his right hand, moving it in a circular motion around his shoulder.

"I am now disconnecting your left arm from the rest of your body. You now have no control of your left arm. The more you try to move it, the less it will move." José then brought Dr. R. out of the state, repeating, "You will not be able to move your arm. One, two, three. Eyes open."

José asked for volunteer doctors to come on stage to examine Dr. R. as they would any patient who complained of an inability to move an arm. Each encouraged Dr. R. to move his left arm, but he would substitute his right arm, saying, "I really cannot move it."

After the doctors had convinced themselves of the reality of the paralysis, José put Dr. R. into another hypnotic state and reversed the suggestion. "Your left arm is now normal." When he came out, Dr. R. easily obeyed instructions to move his left arm.

"You see," explained José, "the problem was not physical in origin so it would not respond to conventional or orthodox methods of healing."

José then went through the same procedure, but this time he created a spastic type of paralysis. He had Dr. R. hold a pencil in his left hand, wrapping his fingers around it. Then he delivered this hypnotic suggestion: "The more you try to release the pencil, the tighter around it your fingers will get." Again, no doctor could get Dr. R. to release the spastic paralysis. When the suggestion was reversed, the pencil dropped from Dr. R's hand.

Some doctors in the audience raised some questions on anesthesia. José answered by again demonstrating on Dr. R. He put the doctor under hypnosis and traced a line on his wrist with his finger. "From this line forward, your hand will become numb and insensitive to pain. Your hand is becoming colder and colder. It feels like it's made of wood. It's insensitive to touch."

Doctors came up and tested the hand. One placed the arm behind Dr. R.'s back so he could not see what was happening. He then inserted the point of a pin under his fingernail. There was no flinch. He then pricked his wrist above the line. Dr. R. flinched, saying, "You pricked me."

The audience was amazed. José ended with a brief on this "God-given" method of pain control, explaining its potential.

"What do we do now?" asked one physician, "Go back to medical school and start over?"

"No," said José, "hire technicians skilled in these approaches." Applause, drinks, and snacks followed. The atmosphere was cordial, even enthusiastic, but even today few technicians skilled in hypnosis are employed in the medical world.

José heard later that the wife of one of the doctors had contracted cancer. He offered to help. "Thanks," said the doctor. "I'll call you."

He never did.

Chapter 7
Following Jesus

In 1963, José started to experiment with training groups of twenty people simultaneously in clairvoyance rather than one at a time. He worked with groups of each sex, accelerating the training, and by 1965 he was satisfied that he could develop clairvoyance successfully in both group and individual settings.

Still, he was spending a great deal of time and money in his training efforts and reaping only experience. So he wrote a letter to President Lyndon B. Johnson, offering to turn over all his research to the government, no strings attached. "I feel it is my duty to God and my country and to all humanity to turn over to you, or to persons assigned by you, all information accumulated to date relative to the knowledge of how to develop the paranormal faculties of the human mind."

A reply arrived about three weeks later from the associate director of research at the National Science Foundation. The director acknowledged José's letter to the president but in effect said, "Thanks, but no thanks."

Some time later, a minister who became a skilled clairvoyant as a result of training was discharged by the head of his congregation "for investigating the powers of the mind." It came as no news to José to find that closed minds were not limited to the national level but were to be found at the grass roots level as well.

Another man who took the training publically announced he had joined the training to expose it, since he had been told José was working for the devil. This man was a Grand Knight in the Nuevo Laredo Knights of Columbus. He later became José's first instructor of the Silva Method in the Spanish language.

As José's confidence and experience grew, the local environment became more difficult to work in. Townsfolk and even fellow churchgoers accused José of working for the devil. It became obvious that neighbors and friends were staying away, clearly intent on having nothing to do with him, with Paula, or with their children. Many even went so far as to cross the street to avoid the Silva home. During sermons in church, priests would recommend to the congregation that they avoid Silva's trainings. "His work," they asserted, "has to do with the devil."

José could not help thinking of the leaders of an established church two thousand years earlier who had accused Jesus of the same thing.

How could learning to use one's God-given intelligence be of the devil? The very accusations meant to discourage him set José to considering how the mental powers he was uncovering related to Jesus' teachings.

José had found that animal, or biological, intelligence functions on five cycles brain frequency and that human intelligence functions best on ten cycles brain frequency. Even to this day, scientists have not fully arrived at this point in their progress. Their biggest obstacle is the scientific method, which requires repetitive consistency in experimental results.

Owing to several factors, in the area of the mind such protocol does not apply. One factor is the presence of the scientist's own mind. In Newtonian physics, the scientist could be an objective observer, but in Einsteinian physics, the scientist's mind introduces another variable: the scientist's own expectation and belief.

José did not have to cope with his own mind as a variable. It was already at a high level of expectation and belief.

Another factor still creating confusion among scientists is their inability to separate the two brain hemispheres in lab experiments. Feedback between the two erases their separate characteristics.

Since José's efforts were aimed at pragmatic uses, when problems were solved, whether creatively, intuitively, or psychically, that was the only kind of feedback he sought.

So, as the scientists have struggled for these past decades in quagmires of their own making, José has moved ahead.

The ten cycles brain frequency exists at the center of the alpha dimension, as explained earlier, the human brain's strongest, most stable frequency. Since human intelligence and mind are subjective—that is, invisible, intangible, and nonphysical—their domain is also a subjective, intangible, nonphysical dimension.

When humans learn to slow down their brain activity in order to function at ten cycles brain frequency, not only are they learning to use the subconscious consciously, but they are also learning to use the right brain hemisphere consciously.

They are learning to use the center of human intelligence, the inner consciousness, for the solution of problems. José mused about problem solving being our ultimate purpose on earth. He was convinced that each brain hemisphere has its own set of sensors. The left brain hemisphere has a set of physical sensors and the right brain hemisphere has a set of mental sensors. All information perceived with the physical sensors is impressed on the left brain hemisphere and is transferred and impressed on the right brain hemisphere. The information perceived by the mental sensors is impressed on the right brain hemisphere, but is *not* transferred to the left brain hemisphere.

Physical information is impressed on the left brain hemisphere at twenty cycles brain frequency. Mental, or subjective, information is impressed on the right brain hemisphere at ten cycles brain frequency.

José's years of research convinced him that when a person's awareness is functioning at ten cycles, that person is aware not only of the impressions made on the right brain hemisphere but also of the information impressed on the left brain hemisphere. When a person is functioning at twenty cycles, that person is only aware of information impressed on the left brain hemisphere and is not aware of the information impressed on the right brain hemisphere. This means that one can solve more problems when functioning at ten cycles, using the inner conscious right brain hemisphere.

José concluded that the wisdom of "turning off" the outside world and going within corresponded with Jesus' references to the kingdom of heaven within us. Jesus had added that even if they say it is here or there do not believe them, the kingdom of heaven is within you. Seek that kingdom and function within God's righteousness and everything else will be added unto you. By learning to use their right hemispheres, human beings come to use the subconscious consciously and to enter the kingdom of heaven.

Eventually, José's teachings took on the form of what is known in theological circles as natural theology. But from his point of view, natural theology is nothing more than plain common sense. As José explains it, when you understand the kingdom of heaven in terms of actualizing potential brain power, the sayings of Jesus not only make sense but also serve a practical purpose: They aid in solving problems.

As he studied the teachings of Jesus more intensely in those days, José came to realize that, besides Jesus, only Matthew, of all the disciples, used the term *kingdom of heaven* to refer to the dimension of wisdom and prophecy Jesus was encouraging the disciples to enter. All the other disciples called that same dimension the *kingdom of God*. The distinction, José understood, was no accident. The kingdom of heaven, he realized, could be reached by going within, while the kingdom of God could be reached only after dying.

In chapter 4, verse 17, Matthew quotes Jesus as saying, "Repent, for the kingdom of heaven is at hand." José's interpretation of this verse is: "Take notice. Everybody can now reach the dimension where many problems can be solved."

José was sure, as he prepared to go public with his training, that Jesus was directly responsible for the progress he was making in his research into the human brain.

How could he ignore the appearance of *One Solitary Life,* or the dry picture of Jesus that arrived in a rainstorm at a critical moment? How could he ignore the white light in his head that surrounded a vision of that picture and all the "coincidences" that had led to the lottery prize? How could he ignore his poverty and his need to contend with the material world in preschool years, and the fact that, owing to his lack of formal schooling, his right brain never became deadened as it is in most students? There was no doubt in José's mind, when he looked back on his life to that point, that he was doing what he was born to do and that the job was important enough to warrant divine help. In his certainty, he saw that he could, and determined he would, serve as a bridge between science and spirituality.

At the present writing, as Einsteinian physics leads us closer to the idea that there exists an energetic, intelligent basis to the material world, the no-man's-land between science and religion is shrinking. In the 1960s, however, that separation between the realms of religion and science had yet to be crossed. Thus, even by talking to religious people about his natural theology—what he saw as the common sense between his own ideas and those of Jesus—José became embroiled in controversy.

In 1972, José spoke at the University of Puerto Rico. There, José compared his work to work that Jesus himself had done. "He, Jesus, was a master in his field," said José. "It was Christ who said, 'I send you prophets and wisemen.' He also said, 'There is nothing concealed that will not be disclosed and nothing hidden that will not be made known.' Christ was healing with the power of the mind. Christ could do away with pain. Christ could stop bleeding in himself and others."

There was an uneasy rustling in the audience as José continued.

"We who practice the Silva Method believe we are doing exactly that—learning to stop pain and bleeding, healing with our minds, discovering the concealed, and coming to know the hidden. We are also perceiving—clairvoyantly—solutions to current and future problems. In short, we are doing just what he said we could do if we believed in him. And I do believe in him."

Suddenly a man in the audience stood up and raised his hand high above his head to ask a question. José usually answered questions at the end of a lecture, but this man's body language expressed an earnest need to speak.

"Yes, sir?" said José.

The man repeated what José had said about Christ, and added, "I have a question. Why, I ask you, did he bleed and suffer pain on the cross?"

Everyone in the audience seemed to stop breathing.

Silently, José considered the question, but his thoughts were broken into by an explicit message that had its roots in the Bible: "Do not prepare what you are to say; it will come to you when you need it." So he simply began to answer the man. "Thank you for that question," replied José. "To me, the greatness of

Christ was manifested when he chose to suffer like any common being though he really didn't have to."

The silence held for a moment. Then it was shattered by a
thunderous applause. The man, who had seemed very tall, now
looked small. José felt badly about seemingly diminishing him.
He had not wanted to make the man feel ridiculous.

Later, he learned that the man who asked the question was
the dean of the Puerto Rico seminary. He eventually took the
Silva Method training and became a clairvoyant.

By 1966, José had decided that he could invest no more time
or money in research. Counting money he had lost in devoting
time to research instead of business, plus travel, course tuition
for his assistants and himself, and other out-of-pocket expenses,
he had already invested half a million dollars in developing the
method. He considered that money not his but his family's.
Nevertheless, he felt he had no choice but to continue his mind
development work. He knew that he was really just beginning.
The government had refused his offer of the training as a gift.
(A politician told him later, "You should have asked for thirty
million dollars — you would have gotten it.") Now, to recoup his
investment and make the benefit of his discoveries generally
available, José decided to take the method directly to the public himself — to offer the training, for a fee, to anyone with an
interest.

He had reduced the training time to about thirty-eight hours.
Now he added a ten-hour safety factor, just to be sure that no
one would fail to become clairvoyant. He named the resulting
forty-eight-hour course Silva Mind Control and divided it into
four days, numbered and titled as follows:

MC101CR — Controlled Relaxation
MC202GSI — General Self-Improvement
MC303ESP — Effective Sensory Projection
MC404AESP — Applied Effective Sensory Projection

These divisions in the training enabled anybody who had to interrupt the training prior to completion to come back later to
finish it.

Next, materials were prepared and personnel primed to assist.

The only thing missing was the starting whistle. It was only a matter of time and the right opportunity.

One day, the district attorney called José and asked him to come to his office. The two had known each other from childhood, so when the secretary ushered him into the office, they greeted each other by first names.

"José, I'll get right to the point. There's a complaint against you."

"What did I do now?"

"A doctor complained that you healed one of his patients. He says you are practicing medicine without a license. What's going on?"

José explained his approach to healing. "It's more like praying than practicing medicine," he said.

His friend, the district attorney, confided, "Look, this doctor doesn't actually have a case against you. If the patient complained, *then* there would be a case against you. But the patient will not complain. In fact, this patient is grateful for being healed."

As it turned out, José had not even been aware of this particular case. The patient, who had been getting two injections a week to correct a medical condition, had attended a Friday night meeting. After he participated in the mental relaxation exercises, the condition disappeared. Later, this man's doctor met the patient in town. "Why did you stop coming for your injections?" the doctor asked the patient.

"Because they healed me at the Silvas'" was the reply. The complaint to the district attorney was the next step.

Some of the district attorney's own relatives had themselves been attending the Friday night sessions, and they invited him to speak on how to proceed with the healings without getting into legal trouble with the medical profession.

Nevertheless, hassles from the medical world continued to assail the center. One night, José was dining with his family in a crowded restaurant. A cigar-smoking doctor walked in with his wife and, spotting José at a table, jauntily rotated the cigar in his mouth and called out, "Hey, Silva! Still practicing medicine without a license?" Then he let out a bellowing laugh.

"If my wife had not been present," recalled José, "the incident might have ended very differently."

One day José received a phone call from a friend who operated a gasoline station in Laredo near José's house. This man, Mr. R., asked if José would come to his home right away. When José arrived, he could see that Mr. R.'s wife was quite ill. She had a skeletal pain that was ruining both her sleep and appetite. She had quit her teaching job and was losing a lot of weight. The best doctors and clinics had not been able to help. The family doctor in Laredo had recommended she see José Silva.

José explained to the couple what he did.

"Whatever you do," interrupted Mr. R., "will you take the case?"

"Of course," replied José. He did a healing and then repeated it twice, three days apart. Mrs. R. improved immediately and regained perfect health. She was able to resume her teaching job. The problem did not return.

But the case was not over.

Mrs. R. was a good Catholic. She went to a priest for confession. During one such session, she confessed that she allowed herself to be helped by one who works for the devil.

José got a call a few days later from the monsignor.

"Silva, when are you going to stop defrauding people and doing things that God does not like?"

"What things, monsignor?"

"Committing the sin of superstition and getting involved in the supernatural."

There were more accusations. When the monsignor finished, José asked, "Monsignor, how do you know so much about me? Have you come to our meetings?"

"I do not have to go to your meetings to know what you're up to," replied the monsignor.

José knew then that the priest must have heard of his healing in a confession. "Father," he explained, "finding hidden information is *our* field of research. What method are you using? Do you have psychic abilities?"

"I sent spies to your meetings. That's how I know," replied the monsignor, refusing to admit he heard of the practice in confession, and thus breached the code of confidentiality.

"Father, you don't have to send spies to our meetings. We have no secrets. The doors are always open to everyone, especially to priests."

"Silva, you could be excommunicated for what you are doing. We have set a date to meet with you and discuss your situation." He told José the date and hung up. Excommunication meant being banned from the church.

José had many friends who were priests. He told some of them what had happened, and they urged him to let them accompany him to the meeting. "Thanks, but this is something I must do by myself. If I need you, I'll give you a call."

José arrived at the meeting fifteen minutes early. Three monsignors were present to discuss his case. The first started the proceedings. "You, Mr. Silva, have been dealing in fraud, doing things that God does not like, committing the sin of superstition, and getting involved in the supernatural. We have proof from other sources that agree with what we have just said, and this evidence may be enough to justify our request that you be excommunicated."

The monsignor then handed José a letter to read, hinting that there were others. The letter, from a well-known Laredo lawyer, asked, "When are we going to get rid of these cranks?"

José put the letter down and said, "Monsignor, if this is the kind of proof you have, I'm not worried. This is pure hearsay, because this man has never even been to one of our meetings." José then turned his attention to the accusations.

"Now, as to your accusations," he continued, "I would like to get some things straight in my mind. Before I address each point in turn I want to be sure I understand what excommunication means. Does it mean that I will not be allowed to practice the sacraments?"

"That is correct," one of the priests replied.

"And does it mean that, when I die, I will not be buried in a Catholic cemetery?"

Again the answer was "Correct."

"Then I think I understand what is meant by excommunication," he said. "Now, let me tell you monsignors something." José felt no fear. He was voicing his sincere beliefs.

"At one time in my life, I wondered why I was a Catholic. Was it because my parents were Catholic? Suppose my parents were Catholic by mistake; I would then be propagating their mistake. Because of this concern, I took it upon myself to study the origins of the religions. I studied how each religion was started—by whom, for what reasons, and under what conditions. What I found," he told the monsignors, "was that all religions are good. I realized that the main purpose of a religion is to enhance the spiritual factor in the human being, the characteristic that separates us from the other animals. It is through the spiritual factor that we recognize our association with our Creator, God."

The monsignors sat transfixed. It seemed nobody had ever talked to them like this.

"I also understood enough to recognize the difference between human intelligence and biological intelligence," José continued. "I understood that human intelligence and mind function spiritually, in a spiritual dimension. And it is through human intelligence and mind functioning in a spiritual dimension that we can enhance the spiritual factor."

The monsignors looked at each other and appeared not to understand what José had just said. He continued. "Now, all religions are good," José went on, "because they do their best to enhance the spiritual factor of the human being. The only thing we need to watch out for is their representatives."

Then José asked the monsignors, "Is religion for the human mind, or for the human body?"

The monsignors looked at each other again, and one replied, "The human mind."

"All right," said José, touching his head with both hands. "Since I have concluded that all religions are roads to the same God, whether we believe it or not, and my religion is as good as any other, I have decided with my human intelligence and my mind to remain a Catholic and die as a Catholic, whether you monsignors, the bishop, or the pope like it or not. So excommunication does not frighten me. You do what you need to do."

But José did not rest his case there. He was just warming up. "Now, regarding the next subject," he continued, "you mentioned that I was dealing in fraud. How can I defraud anybody when I have served everybody free of charge?" he asked.

"The second thing you mentioned was that God did not like what I was doing," he went on. "My question is: Just how did you monsignors happen to know that God did not like what I am doing? Do you have a direct line with God? If so," José said, "call God right now and see what he says. I'll wait right here." He folded his arms.

The monsignors looked at each other. Then José continued, "I cannot perceive the Creator not wanting me to patch up and correct problems of creation along with alleviating the suffering of creatures.

"Let's consider the third thing you mentioned. You said I was committing the sin of superstition. As I understand it, I would be committing the sin of superstition if I believed in, delved in, or attributed to myself supernatural powers that I do not have. But I am a common human being. I have *never* believed that I was delving into the supernatural. I believe that the ones who are committing the sin of superstition are the ones who are *saying* I'm delving into the supernatural. *They* are the ones who are attributing to me powers that I do not have."

The monsignors sat entranced. It had been a long time since they had been preached to.

"Now, let's go into the fourth thing mentioned here: delving into the supernatural. Do any of you know what parapsychology is?"

They shook their heads.

"Well," he said, "parapsychology may well draw the line between supernormal and supernatural. At this point, existing science cannot yet do that. In any event, since you are completely unfamiliar with parapsychology, you monsignors are simply not qualified to pass judgment on my actions in this field."

The monsignors nodded their heads in agreement. Then José added, "Please, please stop harassing me. I have a lot more to do in this area, so please leave me alone! My work in this area is very difficult, and I surely do not need these additional problems to worry about."

A monsignor made the sign of the cross, saying, "May God

bless you. If this is what God wants, nobody is going to be able to stop you."

"That is what I believe, and nobody is ever going to be able to stop me. Thank you," answered José. "Good-bye, and may God bless you also."

These monsignors never bothered José again, and he has remained an active member of the Catholic church. From that time on, no priest ever accused José of working for the devil. In fact, many began to take part in the work. Today, thousands of priests, ministers, rabbis, nuns, and clergy of all religions have been trained by the Silva Method, and many have helped to train others.

Chapter 8
Going Public:
Psychics, UFOs, and Artists

In the latter half of the 1960s, when the Silva Mind Control Method was about to be launched publicly, José did not have the scientific resources available to him that exist today.

- There were no ongoing projects exploring the ways in which psychological practices might extend life.
- There were no conferences on how the brain affects our emotions and behavior and how this link might be a key to world peace.
- There were no scientific studies on such phenomena as "remote viewing," demonstrating the human ability to sense or perceive stimuli at long distances.
- Little was known about the dangers of stress and the successful management of stress. Biofeedback was in its infancy. Any understanding of the healing power of belief and expectancy was limited to work with placebos.
- Guided imagery to enhance healing was hardly a gleam in a single physician's eye, much less a medical practice. And the term *psychoneuroimmunology* had yet to be coined.
- Finally, mind programming was limited to hypnotic techniques and self-hypnotism, both considered controversial and unscientific.

To expand his knowledge, José Silva had to go where the action was. And his quest did not always take him to places held in high professional repute.

For one thing, he decided to locate and study people who worked with crystal balls to discover exactly what they did to uncover hidden knowledge. He also studied people who worked with cards, tea leaves, pendulums, automatic writing, astral projection, aura reading, and Ouija boards.

He found that crystal ball gazers, tea leaf readers, and those who told fortunes with cards all used these objects as focal points for staring or gazing in a way that defocused their vision and permitted them to enter another thinking dimension. This dimension was called psychic functioning. In studying automatic writing, pendulum work, and Ouija boards, José found that the defocusing of vision helped the psychic practitioners transfer energy to the nerves that control muscle movement and thus enable the information perceived psychically to be manifested physically.

José also investigated mediums, attending their séances and observing their procedures. He deplored the fact that many frauds existed, but gained more knowledge about psychic functioning from each genuine practitioner.

In exploring these shadowy realms, José often heard clairvoyants speaking in generalities that he simply could not confirm. To avoid these frustrating encounters, he devised his own projects with clairvoyants in which the results could be confirmed. In one such situation, he gave a medium detailed guidelines for conducting a séance. Then he gave a duplicate copy of these guidelines to a recently trained Silva Method clairvoyant and assigned the latter the same case. José attended the séance.

"The spiritualist medium I was working with," he recalled, "was a forty-four-year-old woman. The séance took place at night, and the room was lit with a small red lightbulb. When she started to work, the medium began to tremble, groan, sweat, and roll her eyes upward. Her assistant motioned for us to remain quiet. When the medium stopped trembling and straightened up, she said in a different tone of voice, 'What can I do for you, sir?'

"I then gave her the case and asked for the information I wanted. The spiritualist clairvoyant was very thorough in explaining everything in fine detail. When she had finished working with the project, she went into her ritual once again before coming out of her trance."

The following day, José compared the medium's report with that of the Silva-trained clairvoyant. Both reports were identical even in the smallest details. José realized from this close correspondence that the trembling and groaning ritual was unnecessary. The medium explained it by saying that it represented the entrance of another spirit, usually of a deceased person, into the body. Though unnecessary in the Silva Method, the ritual is considered benign. "If whatever you do helps humanity and solves problems," says José, "do it any way you can."

In studying what was termed astral projection, José concluded that this practice was actually mental. When working at a distance to heal a sick person, a Silva-trained clairvoyant is able to describe the patient's immediate surroundings as vividly as would an astral traveler. For example, one Silva practitioner who worked on the health of a year-old baby at a distance of fifteen hundred miles in the case cited earlier described the baby's red hair, adding, "There's a small table next to the bed. On the table there is a unique ashtray made of twisted metal." This information was later confirmed by the adult owner. Reports of many details, such as cracks in bricks, broken mirrors, and other environmental details, routinely were confirmed in even the earliest instances of remote healing. From this, José concluded that what was called astral projection was actually the vivid experience of mental projection.

José found that many cases of trance-state healing were accompanied by the medium's statement, "This is all you need to be in perfect health. From now on you are going to be in perfect health." Could it be that all of the loss of control in trance-like states were unnecessary and that it was the verbal affirmation, by dint of its "programming," that was doing the healing work?

In the Silva Method, both patient and healer maintain full awareness, and "programming" by word and picture does the healing work.

As the slow, step-by-step progress proceeded toward limited acceptance of the Silva Method in academic and scientific circles, one of the biggest challenges to the Silva Method came from within José's own family.

José learned that his brother Juan had a health problem. He would occasionally swell up and look like a balloon. It was a painful situation that involved a fever and the occurrence of blue patches and spots. Juan is six feet, two inches tall, large boned, and on the heavy side. "When he swelled up, he looked like a monster," recalls José.

Juan did not believe in what his brother was doing. "José is studying to be a witch doctor," he would joke, adding, "but a modern witch doctor—he won't ride a broom to make his calls; he'll use a vacuum cleaner."

When the frequency of the swelling attacks increased from once a month to once a week and the veterans hospitals could offer no relief, José decided to brave a visit to Juan. He knew he could help Juan at a distance, but if he did that his brother would attribute his cure to other factors. José wanted Juan to know what could be done his way.

José visited Juan at his exporting business office and was introduced to a customer from Mexico, who was also an old friend of Juan's.

Turning to his brother, José asked, "How are you getting along with that health problem?"

"I just got over an attack yesterday," Juan replied, "and it looks like another one is coming on. I may have to go home early."

"Buddy, you've been suffering from that for several years, and you've always rejected my offer to help. Maybe you don't want to lose your government disability pay."

"What kind of help?" asked the friend.

Juan slapped his knee. "I've gone all around the world looking for specialists to cure me. It's service related, and medical doctors with the rank of colonel and general have tried and failed. Yet José, with no medical training whatsoever, thinks he can help me!"

"Wait a minute, Juan," interrupted his friend. "Is your brother going to charge you?"

"No."

"Well, what have you got to lose? One, you'll find out if he can help you. Two, you'll get him off your back!"

"You know, that makes sense." Juan turned to José. "All right, when do you want to do your thing?"

"Right now," replied José.

"You mean right here, right now?"

"Well, we could have more privacy in your office," José suggested.

"Can I watch?" asked the friend. José agreed. Once inside Juan's office, the friend asked, "Can you help me, too? I've had migraine headaches since I was a child."

"All right," José said. "Then what I say goes for the two of you." It was the first time he would try to heal two people in the same session at the same time. "No interruptions, no questions until later."

He used the confusion technique to lower their critical faculty defenses, talking nonsense for about an hour. He exploited their confusion from time to time by programming first one and then the other. He concluded with the standard instructions: "All you need to do is get yourself a glassful of water at night. You personally get it, don't let anyone else get it for you. Drink half the water before going to bed, and the other half first thing in the morning when you wake up." To his brother, he added, "Let me know about any unusual experience that takes place in the next three days."

Nothing happened on the first or the second mornings, but on the third morning, José received a phone call from Juan at 7 A.M. "Come over quickly."

When José arrived, Juan said, "Sit down. Be comfortable. You wanted to know about any unusual experience. Well, I had one this morning."

Juan then related how he awoke at four that morning with the worst swelling yet. He had a high fever and could hardly open his eyes. His wife wanted to call an ambulance.

"Wait," he told her. "My witch doctor brother said something unusual was going to happen. This might be it." In a few minutes, the swelling started to recede and the fever dropped. Fifteen minutes later, the attack was over.

"I was completely clean—cleaner than ever before. No blue spots on my arms and behind my knees. José, I feel as though I am cleared of the swelling problem forever."

And he was right. He never had another attack. Of course, he became a believer in his brother's work. Juan Silva went to work shortly after that as general manager of a factory in Mexico City, and there he eventually taught the Mind Control Method. Twelve years later, Juan resigned from the factory to join Mind

Control full-time and become its director of foreign operations. At this writing, he remains in that position, facilitating the expansion of millions of superminds in seventy-nine countries.

What about his friend with the migraine? That man soon forgot the meaning of the word.

Although it gave José great personal satisfaction, the days, months, and years of debunking and being debunked did not end with the conversion of his brother. Indeed, they may never end, as the functioning of the brain's right hemisphere continues to be the "black sheep" of a left-brain world.

By staying open to the method's possibilities, José found ways to enter into the public realm. In an incident in Amarillo, Texas, for example, a man I will call Mr. A.O. claimed he had been on a trip aboard a UFO. *Time, Life,* and *Newsweek* magazines all sent reporters, photographers, and artists to the site. The latter drew little green men with slanted eyes and the vehicle Mr. A.O. reported to have ridden in.

José offered to use hypnosis to check Mr. A.O.'s story. He regressed Mr. A.O. to one day before the event and then moved him forward minute by minute, comparing the results with Mr. A.O.'s initial report. José was meticulously thorough both in inducing hypnosis, using standard methods, and in testing the depth of the trance. For the latter, he used a well-known test involving a small bottle of gardenia perfume and another of ammonia. The subject is told that the ammonia is actually rose perfume, and after deeply inhaling each is asked which he prefers. Unhypnotized people are unable to inhale the noxious fumes of ammonia deeply, so when the subject seems to enjoy the ammonia and replies, "This rose perfume is not bad, but I like the gardenia better," the depth of the hypnotic trance is confirmed.

Mr. A.O.'s description under hypnosis of his U.F.O. varied in significant ways from his previous account. For instance, he reported that he took a paperweight from a desk as a souvenir of the spacecraft. One of the crewmen discovered what he had done and hit him on the back of the head, causing him to fall.

"How is it that you fell backward if you were hit on the back of the head?" José asked.

"I don't know."

"And if you had fallen backward, then your feet would have been nearest the exit and you would have been taken out feet first. Is that the way it happened?" Previously, Mr. A.O. had said he was carried out head first. Now he replied, "I cannot tell you because, you see, I was unconscious." This was the key to unmasking Mr. A.O.'s fraudulent claims, since, as José well knew, hypnotized subjects are fully capable of relating events that took place while they were unconscious.

At first, José's discovery of the hoax was ignored, but, under continued pressure by journalists, Mr. A.O. finally confessed to lying. José got the news on the car radio one night as he drove from Lubbock, Texas, to Amarillo. "The Soviet Union has decided to discontinue its UFO investigations due to the Amarillo UFO hoax." Although his own contribution went unacknowledged, José felt that his participation in an event with international ramifications confirmed the significance of his efforts.

At a lecture at Wayland Baptist College, Dr. N. E. West, chairman of the Social Science Divison noted, "José precipitated a marked renewal of interest in parapsychological research, particularly in connection with the use of hypnosis." It was at this event that Mr. Dord Fitz invited José to come to Amarillo to lecture members of the Area Arts Association.

José views that invitation as marking the official birth of the Silva Mind Control Method. "When I think about my life, it seems that it has always been guided and directed by some force. This force knows what I need to do and I have always been receptive to it. By that I mean that I have never struggled to hold on to the past. When one business venture slowed down, another was waiting for me. We encountered many obstacles, but were able to overcome every one.

"The invitation of the Arts Association was the work of this force. The association was an ideal place to bring my work to the public in a manner that would be self-supporting and ensure its growth. Artists use more of the right brain hemisphere as they visualize and create ideas. It was a natural thing that artists were to move to the next step: using the right brain hemisphere clairvoyantly. The force used the path of least resistance."

Experiencing the Silva Mind Control training today, one would never suspect that it evolved from hypnosis. In hypnosis, the subject relinquishes control to the hypnotist. With the Silva Method, the subject is always in control. The subject can accept or reject anything that the lecturer says—a far cry from hypnosis.

However, back in the early 1960s, scientific leaders in the field of the mind were confined largely to the field of hypnosis. It provided the only direct scientific entry into deeper levels of the mind. As a result, José's research began with hypnosis, and when he started teaching it was an advanced course in hypnotism. This was before the Silva Method.

But all the while, he was seeking to extract from the hypnotic techniques ways to place the subject in control and ways to adapt medical applications of hypnosis to educational ends. In hypnosis, there are authoritarian approaches and permissive approaches. By focusing his research on total permissiveness and self-control, José was able to evolve his teachings away from authoritativeness, medical uses, and heterocontrol in the direction of permissiveness, education, and self-control.

By 1963, José had trained thirty-nine subjects in psychic functioning using permissive hypnotism. By 1966, when he received the invitation to speak to the Arts Association in Amarillo, he had succeeded in developing the Silva Method, freeing it from its hypnosis origins and enabling trainees to maintain conscious control of their levels of awareness. The key was a series of conditioning cycles from which the trainee could derive deep levels of relaxation and the benefits of mental programming under conscious control.

All of this work was confined largely to Laredo, Texas, and the other side of the Rio Grande in Nuevo Laredo, Mexico.

The trip to Amarillo would prove to be not only a geographical breakthrough but the start of an educational breakthrough that promises to enlighten the planet.

José invited a colleague to join him on the trip to the Arts Association. This was his number one helper at the Friday night sessions in Laredo. He shared in the donations, after expenses, at those sessions. He had joined José on other research and training trips, and José had always paid his expenses.

"How much are we going to get paid?" he asked.

"Nothing," replied José. "They are paying only my expenses, but I will pay your expenses myself." The colleague refused to go. Soon after, he broke off relations with José, started an activity of his own, then quit altogether.

When José stepped into that meeting room in Amarillo, he faced ninety artists, and he had a hunch: At age fifty-two, he was launching into a completely new career.

By the end of his talk — on tapping right-brain resources — his hunch had been confirmed. Almost all the artists in the room signed a request that he return to Amarillo to teach them to become clairvoyants. All were willing to pay for the training. This would be the first time in José's twenty-two years of research that he would receive remuneration for training clairvoyants.

A few days later, Dord Fitz, the director of the center, wrote to José: "We have had many famous people lecture at the Dord Fitz Art Center, but we have never had a speaker hold an audience so spellbound before. . . . For those of us in the creative arts, the creative act is a semiconscious act and related to clairvoyance. Music flows through us, great paintings, poetry, and so on flow through and become physical manifestations to be shared consciously with all who desire them.

"We must, of course, train ourselves under great teachers to master the technical skills, that they may become automatic and serve us when the semiconscious state we call inspiration takes hold of us. We must have had training to become discerning persons knowing the greatest taste and quality in our fields.

"I feel that your discovery to the effect that under deep concentration a human being becomes clairvoyant is one of the great mind discoveries. All artists will certainly want the training you can give, and of course we already know of the benefit to doctors and other professional people."

José started the artists' training on a Friday night in October and completed it in January 1967. Almost immediately, another course was assembled, this one formed of friends and relatives of graduates of the first. Soon word spread to Lubbock, and that city became a regular training spot for José. Other cities were to follow in the months ahead.

At the first meeting, a student asked José to name other applications of the clairvoyant ability besides healing.

"For doing anything that is constructive and creative more fully" was José's reply.

"To improve one's painting?"

"Of course. Do you want to paint better?"

When the woman answered yes, José helped her get to the relaxed alpha level.

"Who would you like to emulate in your painting?" he asked.

"Van Gogh."

"Fine. Imagine right now that you are painting a copy of a Van Gogh."

The group watched as the woman moved her hands as though painting. When she was finished, José told her, while she was still at her relaxed level, that all she would have to do to get Van Gogh's advice in her future work would be to put her three fingers together and concentrate on the image of Van Gogh.

When she ended her session, José asked her to paint something employing this concept. She did a vase with flowers in it. Just as she was finishing, Mr. Fitz entered to join the meeting. He looked at the painting and began to point out similarities to a Van Gogh. It turned out that this woman was one of the neophytes at the meeting and had had only a few art lessons!

At a future meeting, these same artists told José that they did not want to be copies of anybody, but that they wanted to be creative in their own right.

"Of course," José agreed. "Imitating the great masters is just a good beginning. Why not pick up where they left off?" He then reminded them of what Christ had said. "He who believes in me and the works that I do, he also shall do, and greater than this he shall do."

Many in the class went on to become better artists. Two, Mrs. Sheets and Mrs. Blodgett, both housewives, went on to become Silva instructors. The former is still an active trainer at this writing.

One commerical artist, a Mr. Fujita, who took the training in Amarillo, surprised José with the gift of a large diagram of the inner and outer conscious levels. During class, José had resorted to crude sketches on a chalkboard or on an artist's sketchpad, but this diagram was beautifully rendered in color. The Scale of Brain Evolution, shown on page 11, became a part of the training. Mr. Fujita later moved to Fort Worth, where he organized a Silva training class. Soon, training was regularly scheduled in Fort Worth. In the same way, other graduates established classes in their home cities. Soon José found himself traveling to Dallas, Austin, Fort Worth, and San Antonio.

Sometimes, however, the arrangements did not take hold. One group organizer, Dr. H. of San Antonio, told José that his relatives in Houston would help organize groups there. José gave him a date to work with. Dr. H. arranged a meeting room and sleeping quarters in a Houston motel for that date. When José arrived, the meeting room was ready, but the relatives had gone out of town without placing the advertisement in the newspaper. Nobody knew of the meeting, so nobody came.

However, two ladies passing by the meeting room saw a sign on the door: "Mind Control Lecture." They looked in.

"What is mind control?" one asked.

José did not exactly give his lecture to an audience of two, but he did take the time to explain his method.

Turning to her companion, the first woman, Mrs. D. said, "We must introduce Mr. Silva to . . . "

"Yes," interrupted the other, "Mr. I."

"Right." Turning to José, she said, "Since you are staying overnight, please allow us to take you to Unity Church in the morning to meet the minister, Mr. I."

José agreed, and the next day he met Mr. I and set a date for a lecture two weeks later. Mr. I would announce at every service until then. When José returned, he spoke to a full house. Mrs. D. became the Houston Silva organizer, and her friend, who was a nurse, became her assistant.

Interest in the training increased daily. At a lecture José gave to the graduate students in the Department of Psychology at the University of Texas at Austin, there was standing room only. The organizer noted that never before had so many Ph.D.s come together for such an event.

As José began his talk, using the Scale of Brain Evolution, a voice called out, "Skip the chart explanation. We don't go for theories. We want the real thing!"

Another Ph.D. chimed in, "Skip the chart and give us the meat."

Now other comments began to ring out. "Parapsychology is a lot of bunk." "Give us proof." "Forget the theory."

José, realizing he was in the lion's den and about to be chewed up, recalled the interior message he had once received about allowing the right reply to come to him automatically. He held up his arms toward the audience, palms outward, motioning for quiet.

When the room settled down, the slightly built man from Laredo suddenly had a big voice. "I would like to remind you that I am your guest. Is this the way highly educated people treat their guests?"

He paused. The room became still. Then he asked, "Who in this room has done research in the field of parapsychology? Raise your hand."

Nobody raised a hand.

"I have been researching in parapsychology for twenty-three years. I am the only authority on parapsychology in this room. I am not going to lecture you on psychology. *You* are the authorities in that field. By the same token, you are not going to tell me about my field. Now, about my chart . . . "

José received rapt attention for an hour and a half. The questions that followed were serious and intelligent. He was applauded at the close. "Never before have I seen these Ph.D.s stay riveted so long in their seats," commented the host.

At a dinner given him by the parapsychology club that night, José reminded those in attendance that he had no formal education at all. "If you had known that earlier, you would never have let me step on the campus lawn, much less speak. But it's too late now." Most thought he was kidding.

Houston turned out to be a particularly receptive area for the newly launched Silva Mind Control training. Free lectures, organized by Mrs. D. and her nurse assistant, always yielded a good-sized class. After one of these lectures, a man came over to José. "My name is Harry McKnight. Mrs. D.'s assistant said I might talk with you about a scholarship."

"We give scholarships to all directors of departments of psychology," responded José, voicing a decision he had made earlier.

"I am working on my Ph.D. I am on a small stipend. My wife is expecting. Your lecture has convinced me that I must take the training, but I don't have any money." McKnight had already filled out a registration card.

"Let me see your card."

José examined it, then wrote on it, "Scholarship." He handed it back. "Take it back to Mrs. D. I have approved you for a scholarship."

Harry thanked José and took the card back to Mrs. D. He took the training, joined the Silva organization, and became one of its most valuable assets, the first staff instructor to assist in training groups. In fact, with Harry, José split the territory, which was confined to Texas at the time—assigning Harry half the state and himself the other. Later, Harry developed an instructor's manual for the course that has been in use ever since.

"Giving Harry McKnight a scholarship was one of the best decisions of my life," says José. "And I didn't have to think about it. I didn't have to put him through an extensive interview or testing. I just had a hunch that it was the right thing to do."

At first, Harry began to help José part-time while working on his Ph.D. internship at the Veterans Administration hospital in Houston. But soon his advisor confronted him about his involvement with mind control. "A psychologist cannot be involved in unethical functions," the advisor asserted, and he insisted that Harry choose between one discipline or the other. Harry chose mind control.

Later, Harry helped José expand the training. At first it was difficult for students to accept a substitute for José. In Amarillo, for example, when José announced that Harry McKnight would be taking his place at a forthcoming instructors' training, there was an immediate outcry. "No, we want you."

"Wait a minute," argued José. "If that's the way you want it,

Silva Mind Control will never grow. I can't be the only trainer; I'm saturated already. We need more instructors to reach as many people as possible."

He went on to explain the thoroughness of Harry's training and his exceptional abilities as an educator. "Why not let me send him here? You question him. If you think he's prepared, all right. If not, he won't teach."

Harry made a special trip to Amarillo to see if he would be deemed qualified to teach the method. After a talkfest with him, the potential instructors signed up for the training gave him the okay. So the hundreds of lecturers who now give the training all over the world had as their initiator Harry McKnight. He wrote one of the first books on Silva Mind Control, entitled *Silva Mind Control Through Psychorientology*, he took charge of education cassette tape programs, and he conducted the lecturer training program.

I received my own lecturer training in 1975 from Harry Mc-Knight and Nelda Sheets, one of the artists in the first Amarillo class, and I took the graduate lecture series from both José Silva and Harry McKnight. In my own classes, I have always used something I heard from Harry, and if I have neglected to give him credit for it at any time along the way, let me correct the oversight by giving him the credit now.

When the trainees in clairvoyant healing have completed their cases—that is, when they have correctly described a person a fellow student has presented, identified the person's illness, and corrected it at the creative level, all at an average of 80 percent accuracy—Harry would say, "When you can project your intelligence any distance, which you all were able to do today, that's the quality of being infinite. When you can go forward and backward in time, which some had to do today, that's the quality of being eternal. If you can know things you have no apparent way of knowing—and all of you proved you can do that—that's omniscience. And if you can change unwanted conditions—again, which you all did—that's omnipotence.

"Infinite, eternal, omniscient, omnipotent—who indeed are you?"

Whenever I pose this question in my training sessions, there are always a few students who dare to whisper the answer.

Harry and José later convinced James Needham, a flight instructor in Lubbock, to become the third Silva Mind Control instructor. And in a Laredo restaurant during a training session break, an incident occurred that unexpectedly extended the network across the country. Two men approached José.

"Mr. Silva?"

"Yes."

"We have been looking for you all over. We have just arrived from California. My name is Mr. K. This is my friend, Mr. L. We have heard so much about you, we decided to see if you are for real. We would like to take your training now."

"Impossible," José replied. "I am about to finish this group. Then I go to Mexico City to help our instructors there to get started."

"We'll pay you three times the cost, but we want it now."

"Still impossible," replied José.

"How long will you stay in Mexico?"

"One week. Then I have a week off."

"If you would stay in Mexico during a second week, I will fly a number of people to Mexico City to take the training."

José thought for a moment. "I will need to have twenty people minimum to pay expenses."

"If I pay for twenty," Mr. K. asked, "might I take more—say, thirty—for the same price?"

"Pay for twenty and bring as many as you like," José replied.

More than twenty attended. They were from a cosmetics company in California with a multilevel sales force. When the training was over, they tested each other for clairvoyant ability. Then they paid José. He learned later from Mr. K. that they had intended to withhold payment if they had not become clairvoyant. But the group was satisfied, and several distributors from this special class followed José to Lubbock the following week to attend an advanced Mind Control training session required of graduates interested in becoming lecturer candidates.

Eventually, ten of the distributors from that cosmetics company became Silva Mind Control lecturers. One was assigned to

New York City, one to Buffalo, one to Washington, D.C., one to Pennsylvania, two to Chicago, two to Wisconsin, one to Florida, and one to Boston. Now Silva Mind Control was in place to reach those all across the country who hoped to expand their mental powers and deepen their spiritual lives.

Chapter 9
Reactions: Detractors, Imitators, and Miracles

To no one's surprise, given José's early experience, as the Silva tide spread from coast to coast, it made waves everywhere.

The method and its implications aroused the indignant opposition of professionals and nonprofessionals alike involved in mental research. These objectors were so deeply rooted in the sensory physical world that they were simply unable to give credence to the existence of the extrasensory. So they made waves of conflict.

In some Silva graduates, the new knowledge aroused greed and ego to the extent that they grabbed the ball, claimed it as their own, and ran with it. They made legal waves.

In the beneficiaries of its "miracles," the method aroused wonder and even awe. *They* made public relations waves.

Space here permits a description of only representative events of these kinds. But for each of these examples, similar incidents took place all over the country, contributing to an ocean's worth of energy surrounding the Silva Method.

Between 1966 and 1969, when José was training groups within the state of Texas only, only one article about the training appeared in a national magazine. The author was a sixty-year-old Dallas widow, and the magazine was the 1969 edition of *Woman.* The article conveyed quite a favorable impression of José Silva's work.

The writer had taken only half the training before she wrote the article. She ended the article by saying, "They say I will become a genius when I finish the rest of the training."

"Did she?" José was asked later by a number of readers.

His reply, based on his own follow-up was, "She married a millionaire."

After the training sessions expanded to the rest of the nation, stories in the national media began to proliferate. Nine out of ten articles in those days were negative, suggesting, as one reporter put it, that "Silva is selling snake oil." Today, by the way, in an age of a new and more evolved consciousness, nine out of ten stories are positive.

José was never "thrown" by his detractors, but they got under his skin sometimes. He knew that none had taken the training and that they were writing from ignorance. Still, it disappointed and bothered him to see them mask their ignorance with authority and write as if they knew what they were writing about, damaging others by their untruths.

One day a Catholic priest came to Laredo from Edinburgh, Texas, a small college town near McAllen, with the sole intention of exposing what he felt was Silva's fraudulent operation. When the priest arrived at José's home, he got right to work.

"You, as a Catholic, should be ashamed of yourself, fooling these people by making them believe they can function clairvoyantly," the priest said to José, referring to some of the priest's own parishioners who had taken the training. In a loud voice, he demanded, "If it's true that people can function clairvoyantly, then you prove it to me right here and now!"

Replied José, "Father, first I want to remind you that you are in my house. Second, please remember that priest or not, neither you nor anyone else should talk to me in such a loud voice. Third, I'm under no obligation to prove anything to you. You must understand that it is *you* who is ignorant and that the things I have taught are possible. So it is you who have the problem, not I."

Surprisingly, the priest changed his tone of voice and was most apologetic, asking for forgiveness. Then he said, "Maybe I am the way I am because I have never seen anybody function clairvoyantly. Can you do something that can convince me?"

At that time there was a twelve-year-old girl at José's house who was taking intensive training in clairvoyance. "All right, Father, that's a totally different attitude. Under those conditions I will demonstrate something for you to try to convince you." He then called in the little girl.

"Have you ever seen this little girl before?" he asked the priest.

"No."

"Well, this little girl has had the same training your parishioners have. Would you believe that there is something to what we do if this little girl, not knowing you, tells us something about your life?"

"Yes, if she can do that, that could make me a believer," replied the priest.

The little girl sat in a chair in front of the priest and went to her level of clairvoyance. When she was ready and asked what José wanted her to do, José said, "Give him a general."

"What's a general?" asked the priest.

"It is a check of your general health."

The priest shrugged his shoulders, and the little girl started.

The young clairvoyant started to move her hands in the air as though she were holding something. José asked her, "What are you doing?" and she answered, "I am starting on his head and am now checking his hearing. His hearing through the left ear is weaker than the right." The priest looked at José and shrugged his shoulders.

The little girl worked through the trunk of the body, saying, "He is very healthy." When she got to the groin level, she stopped and said, "Mr. Silva?"

"Yes?"

She continued, "Do you remember that case we worked on where you told us a man's scar meant he had had a hernia operation?"

"Yes, I remember."

The little girl said, "The priest has two, one on each side." The priest looked at José and said, "Is she looking at me?"

"Yes, Father."

The priest gathered his cassock and folded it between his legs. "It's too late, Father. She already knows."

The little girl continued checking the area at the groin level. Then she said, "I'm checking the end of the spinal column. The last bones should all be stuck together, but the last one, the tailbone, is loose."

José looked at the priest and he again shrugged his shoulders, indicating he did not know that his tailbone was loose.

The little girl said, "We'll find out later how and when the little tailbone became loose."

When the little girl reached the priest's feet, she said, "Now I'm going to regress him mentally to when the priest was a baby, and work forward."

She started rotating her hands, as if moving the hands of a clock, using a Silva technique so she could regress and progress him in time in order to tell about his childhood. She told the priest how old he was when he fractured his right knee. She told him when he fell down some stairs. And she told him that the priest was seven years old when his mother died.

A little later, the little girl stopped and said, "It is here when he broke his tailbone. Let's see how it happened." She started to rotate her right hand back and forth, saying, "I see it now. He's riding a horse. The horse throws him, and he lands on some rocks. *That's* how it happened, and because of that he was kept in a hospital for three days."

When he heard that, the priest stood up, holding his head, saying, "Oh, my God, this is the real thing!" He was walking around in circles, giving José an occasional look, and repeating over and over, "This is the real thing! This is the real thing!"

Once the priest quieted down, José said, "You see, Father, if I were to use my time to prove to every disbeliever that this was the real thing, I would not have time to do anything else. You see how long it took to make a believer of you. What did I gain? You took my time, and I gained nothing." The priest left, promising to help any way he could.

Some months later, José was giving a free opening lecture in a motel in McAllen, when the Edinburgh priest appeared at the door.

"Come in, come in," said José.

The priest asked, "Might I say a few words?"

José nodded.

The priest turned to the audience and described his experience in Laredo. "This was the real thing," he added.

Since the priest was well known in the area, everyone in the audience signed up and took the training. So the priest did help in some way, as he had promised.

A Boston woman wrote a scathing article in the *Boston Globe*. "Silva is of the devil" was her theme, and "Fraud!" her exclamation point.

José grabbed the next plane to Boston. He told the editor, "She said we were frauds. Why didn't she pick up the phone and call the Better Business Bureau or our Laredo city officials? And I don't think she talked to the devil either."

The editor agreed to assign another reporter to take the training at the newspaper's expense and to do a story. "Descent Into Alpha" was the result. To this day, the article remains one of the most descriptive and eloquent articles ever written about the Silva Mind Control training.

Harry McKnight and his wife, Laredo, moved from Houston to Laredo when he joined the Silva organization and began a newsletter. The first issue, called *Mind-Control-Communique*, was published in July 1969. Its feature story reported that, in the year and a half since José Silva had given his first lecture in Dallas, eight classes had graduated, producing nearly three hundred clairvoyants.

By contrast, a little over a year later, volume 2, number 1 of the newsletter, now renamed *Mind Control Newsletter*, had this headline on its front page: "FORT WORTH MIND CONTROL CENTER GRADUATES 221." José Silva was present on that evening, December 30, 1970, to address the largest class to date and to commend Hap Arnold, director of the Mind Control Center and instructors Ron Bynum and Mark Loving. The previous record had been 122 students the year before in Mexico.

The greatest threat to Silva Mind Control and its growth came in California. José had taken his eldest daughter, Isabel, to Los Angeles to form the first class there. He scheduled and publicized a lecture at a motel. Isabel gave a demonstration at that lecture of what a clairvoyant could do and thus what those in the audience could expect to do if they took the training.

When Isabel was at her alpha level, José asked, "What would you like her to do?"

A lady raised her hand and said, "I am a painter. I have three paintings and four possible customers. Can she tell me the best painting and to whom I should offer it?"

José agreed it was a good project, and the painter started to describe the first of her works. "Don't tell me," Isabel interrupted. "I will describe them to you. If I am correct, you'll have a way of knowing I'm correct in my choice of customer."

She then described all three paintings in detail. The painter was amazed. "How can she do that?" she kept repeating.

Isabel then told the woman, "Your best painting is the woman holding the baby in her arms. Offer it to the stockbroker."

As the painter continued to express her amazement, José told the group, "What you have seen Isabel do here tonight, *you* will be able to do when you take the training—this and much more."

Thirty-two people signed up.

When José got back to Texas, he turned this California class over to a Mr. G. , who was teaching in Fort Worth but seeking to move to California. Mr. G. trained this first California group. There he met Mr. N., and the two decided to form a joint venture. They altered the Silva training in order to work around the copyright infringement law and changed its name.

José, hearing of the illicit activity, went to California to meet with them. Mr. G. sat on one side of the room and let Mr. N. do all the talking.

"I'm glad to see you, Mr. Silva," began Mr. N. "I've been wanting to talk to you. I hope to persuade you to turn the Silva Mind Control Method over to me. The method is an excellent way to help humanity, and I'm in a better position than you to provide that help."

"In what way better?" asked José.

"I am already set up in fourteen countries with my cosmetics business, and I can quickly expand the teaching activity to wherever I have sales representatives." He rattled off scores of both domestic and foreign areas where his organization had a foothold.

José was impressed. "You are indeed in a better position. So I will make you an offer." Their collective ears went up. "You pay a royalty of fifteen percent of the gross, which is what most publishers pay authors."

Mr. N. replied quickly. "Too much. Suppose I just pay you whatever I can, whenever I can?"

"That doesn't sound very businesslike."

"I'm not going to sign a contract," continued Mr. N. "You know good and well that you cannot copyright this method."

"My legal counsel tells me otherwise," replied José.

"Who do you think you're kidding? I'm going to continue using the method. Get your lawyers to try to stop me!"

José arose. "Mr. N., you and I are not going to fight. Let's let our lawyers fight it out. The one in the right will win." At the door, he turned. "Good day, gentlemen. See you in court."

While José was making plans to sue Mr. N. and Mr. G., trouble arose closer to home. Mr. F., who was José's Austin, Texas, organizer and who had joined the Laredo staff as instructor training coordinator, suddenly made a "takeover" move.

He gave José an ultimatum. "If you want me to continue in my position, name me president of the corporation in your place, turn over to me fifty percent of the corporation stock, and, for starters, I'll take a ten thousand dollars a year increase in my salary."

Such a salary increase would give Mr. F. more than José was earning. Furthermore, the corporation was a limited partnership, owned by his family, who had funded the research for twenty-two years.

José's reply was an emphatic "No!"

"You are forcing me to leave and set up my own organization to present the training," F. warned.

"The training is protected by copyright," José reminded him.

"If a California company can get away with it, so can I." Mr. F. had done his homework. "And remember, if I leave, I will take the instructors with me."

"I cannot accept your terms" was José's reply.

There were twenty-three instructors at that time. Mr. F. left and took seventeen with him. He immediately took over the cities where these instructors were teaching, modified the training superficially, changed the name, and allowed the public to believe that the organization was unchanged.

While José set about training more instructors and winning

back the cities he had lost, he decided it would be more practical to file suit against Mr. F. in Texas rather than pursuing the California case.

José won. Mr. F. and his instructors were enjoined by the court from presenting the plagiarized Silva Method. However, by the end of the trial, only two of the original seventeen instructors were still with him. Meanwhile, José had rebuilt his instructor staff from the six who had remained with him to more than fifty.

While José was fighting the F. case, Mr. N. was killed in a plane crash. All of his mind training operations and his cosmetic company activities were disbanded. Another "judge" had ruled on that case.

But plagiarism had become a plague besetting José. Mr. G. created a spin-off of the spin-off, and continued giving classes. A Mr. O. began teaching another version of the Silva Mind Control Method on the Unity Church circuit. And a Mr. P. started another version.

It all became so confusing that even a skilled consciousness author like Jess Stearn admitted to José that he had given credit to the wrong people. Here is the Silva Method terminology compared side-by-side with the method terminology reported in a Stearn book:

SILVA	SPIN-OFF
To Awake Control	Mental Alarm Clock
Awake Control	Staying Awake Technique
Headache Control	Tension Headache Technique
Dream Control	Dream Technique
Mental Screen	Screen of the Mind
Memory Pegs	Memory Control
Three-Fingers Technique	Finger-and-Thumb Technique
Glass-of-Water Technique	Glass-of-Water Technique
Habit Control	Prompt Action
Projection into Metals	Workshop
Laboratory	Workshop
Counselors	Assistants

José soon learned, however, that while spin-offs continue to come and go, the Silva Method and its "miracles" endure.

A driver has a hunch to stop his car on a dark country road. Around the next bend is a stalled car blocking the way.

A woman causes a cancer remission.

A business manager finds a unique solution to a Catch-22 problem.

A wife reconciles with her husband.

A family solves its financial problem.

The proof of the method is in its results, and the results keep right on accumulating.

Chapter 10
Colliding With the
Scientific Community

The Silva Method emphasizes that clairvoyance is action at a distance—cause and effect totally separated in space. Science abhors action at a distance. And so scientists approached Silva Mind Control with a preconceived bias.

In fact, the word *bias* is too weak to describe the reaction of scientists. A *bias* is an inclination that inhibits impartial judgment. But the scientific stance in the late 1960s and early 1970s did more than inhibit fair judgment; it made a fair look at the Silva Method practically impossible.

Any truth to the method would challenge precepts and paradigms that had survived scientific testing. Scientists simply couldn't admit the idea that it was their work, not the Silva Method, that was out of step.

In a way, José's very first graduate, Isabel, led to one of his first tilts with science. Isabel became a registered nurse and a director of nursing in a county hospital. She also married and had three children. Her husband was José de las Fuentas, known as Pepe, a lieutenant commander in the U.S. Navy. Early in their marriage, Pepe was stationed in Kingsville, Texas, and José used to visit the family there frequently.

Pepe was a nonbeliever. He embraced the scientific method and this prevented him from accepting that his wife could function clairvoyantly. Whenever she did indeed do so, Pepe had another explanation for what happened. Hardly a visit went by when José did not find himself involved in a discussion with Pepe about the possibility of clairvoyance.

One weekend during one of José's visits, Pepe came home from work at lunchtime. He motioned to José to come into a room where they could talk.

"I have a good case for Isabel. If she works on it successfully, it will prove to me that clairvoyance exists and that my wife has it."

107

"What's the case?" asked José.

"Never mind. I'll handle this. You get her."

Isabel and José's wife, Paula, were in the kitchen preparing lunch. José looked in on them.

"Pepe has a case for you to work on, Isabel."

She wiped her hands. "Here we go again, Dad. Each time he tests me, he calls it a coincidence."

"No, dear, this time he says it's a test to end all tests." He led Isabel to the room where Pepe awaited. Pepe had placed two chairs back to back.

"I have set the stage for this test," he told Isabel. "You sit there. I'll sit here. Go to what you call your level and tell me when you're ready."

In a moment, Isabel said, "I'm ready."

Pepe continued. "Isabel, this morning I hurt a finger on one of my hands. Can you tell me which finger it is?" Pepe grabbed his left thumb and held it while his wife did her psychic testing. She touched every finger and thumb twice of both of her hands. Pepe continued to hold onto his left thumb.

"It's the little finger of the right hand," Isabel said finally.

"You're correct," admitted Pepe. "I couldn't fool you. I caught it in a chain this morning and nearly fractured it." Then, turning to José, he said, "*Suegro*," which means "father-in-law," "I agree that Isabel has clairvoyance. But I'm sure she has had it from birth and that it cannot be taught."

"Pepe," replied José patiently, "everybody has clairvoyance, but it's naturally developed in only ten percent of the people. Anybody in the other ninety percent can develop it, if they sincerely desire to."

"Will you train me?" asked Pepe.

"Yes, if you come to Laredo on weekends."

Pepe agreed, and he went through the training. To graduate, he needed to do three cases. José had previously prepared the cases and made detailed copies of them in a notebook. These he placed in the right top drawer of his desk. They contained all the aspects of the illnesses.

After Pepe completed his cases successfully, describing people he did not know and identifying their illnesses with great accuracy, José said, "I want to congratulate you, Pepe. You really were excellent."

"Come on, *Suegro*, you are just saying that. Am I to take your word? Is that how you do it?"

"No, Pepe, I can prove it. Open the right top drawer of my desk, get out the black notebook, open it, and read it."

Pepe could not believe his eyes. "This is unbelievable."

"What do you have to say about clairvoyance and the training?" asked José.

"It truly works," admitted Pepe.

"I want you to know that if you were not my son-in-law, I would not have gone to all this trouble to convince you."

Perhaps it had been a lot of trouble, but José was to realize in the years ahead that this was one of the easiest of his science-oriented conversions.

José was invited to lecture to the medical students at the New Health Center Medical School in the University of Texas at San Antonio. He took his youngest son, Antonio, with him. Dr. S., the head of the department of psychiatry, introduced José.

"José Silva heads up Silva Mind Control, which teaches people to control their brain waves. Here, speaking on that subject, is Mr. Silva."

José had been surprised to see that his talk was scheduled not in one of the university's fine lecture halls but in the laboratory where electroencephalographs (EEG), tape decks, and other kinds of electronic equipment were in a ready state. In his speech, José reviewed the scientific contention that alpha waves are produced by human beings only in a state of reverie. If a person with measurable alpha brain waves did a math problem or described another person by visualization, the conventional wisdom held, the alpha waves would be blocked and beta waves would take their place. He then went on to explain that Silva trainees contradicted the accepted pattern. When he finished his hour and a half lecture, he was applauded by the students.

Dr. S. then arose and remarked, "Your theory is interesting, Mr. Silva, but it is only theory. Proving the theory is something else again. Can you demonstrate with the EEG equipment?"

"I have my own EEG in the car. I trust it. You may connect me to both."

Dr. S. agreed, and while Antonio and some students went to fetch the equipment in José's car, Dr. S. and his students connected José to their machine. They used electrodes that are applied subcutaneously; after cleaning the needles with alcohol, they inserted them under José's scalp.

There José sat with little trickles of blood running down his face and wires pulling him in all directions.

"Are you comfortable, Mr. Silva?" they asked. What a question to ask a person used to the electrodes of his own equipment, which function just as well by gentle surface contact!

With both EEGs in place, José explained that he would produce alpha brain-wave rhythms and that while doing so he would describe Dr. S. and then work a math problem. He predicted that the alpha frequencies would not be blocked, but would continue uninterruptedly.

José went to alpha level and the EEGs recorded alpha both audibly and by printout. He then described Dr. S., and worked a math problem with no interruption to the alpha.

The printouts were checked. There was no doubt that José had done it.

"You are undoubtedly an unusual individual, Mr. Silva," commented Dr. S. "You are like some yogis who spend their lives practicing certain exercises. But this doesn't mean you can teach everybody to control and maintain alpha rhythms."

"Anybody who takes our training can do it," countered José. Then turning to Antonio, he added, "My son, Tony, has taken the training. Would you like to test him?"

Dr. S. welcomed the idea, but Tony, looking at the needle electrodes, did not. Eventually, though, he agreed to be wired up and tested, and he did even better than José.

"You see, one *can* be trained. Tony did better because he is younger. My brain is slightly worn out."

Dr. S. then confirmed the test results. "You have proven your theory correct, Mr. Silva. We had expected a different outcome."

A further project was planned: to see if people who took the training could rid themselves of chronic or migraine headaches.

"However, our names and the name of the medical school shall not be mentioned in any paper, and your name, Mr. Silva, shall not be connected with us in any way."

José agreed, but soon afterwards the University of Texas directors heard of the project and canceled it.

A happier outcome resulted from a project conducted by a Dr. T. from Trinity University, also in San Antonio, using medical students at that campus. The successful control of brain waves by students who took the training was the subject of a technical paper published in a scientific journal in England.

In 1972, the Silva training was given to a girls' school in San Antonio. Word of its success reached a Philadelphia private school, the John H. Hallahan Catholic Girls School, and a priest came down to talk to some of the teachers. He then took the training himself, and decided that it would be beneficial to the students in his school. He asked José for a scholarship to train his students.

"How many?" asked José.

"Two thousand," replied the priest.

José thought a moment. The scholarship would be equivalent to a quarter million dollars. "Agreed," he said.

The school was closed for one week to permit the training of the two thousand teenage girls. José called in a psychologist with a doctorate in education to do the pretraining and posttraining testing, using standardized tests. Silva Method lecturers from throughout the area were brought in to do the actual training.

Halfway through the training, the bishop summoned the priest to his office. José accompanied him and was permitted to attend the meeting. A number of other priests were there.

"You had no right to permit this training to take place," the bishop said sternly.

"I am the superintendent of the school," replied the priest.

"Don't you know that this type of training is dangerous? You should have gotten each parent's permission," admonished the bishop.

"I took the training myself. I investigated its benefits where given elsewhere. I had proof that it was not dangerous, but that it was, instead, beneficial. And, yes, I have gotten permission from every parent except one, and that girl is not in the group."

José was permitted to make a statement. He said, "We Christians are going out of our way to help humanity in the best way we know how. You priests are putting obstacles in our way. That is something to think about."

The priest and José departed, leaving the meeting to debate whether or not to stop the project. "If they stop us, I'll resign as a priest," said the superintendent.

"If you do, you can come with us to train more people," offered José.

"I feel better already," sighed the priest.

But the project was not stopped. The posttesting showed a distinct improvement in the students' personality and learning profiles on many levels, and the Silva training turned out to be a feather in the cap of the priest. However, the priest was not permitted to conduct a follow-up testing planned for a few months after the training. The successful experience at the Hallahan School became a model later for similar educational institution projects.

By the early 1970s, some twenty-five medical doctors, mostly in the Texas area, had taken the Silva training. In 1969, José invited them all to a meeting. A large percentage attended. The purpose of the meeting was to determine if the doctors were willing to go before the American Medical Association and demonstrate the use of clairvoyance in diagnosing and healing.

The decision was no. The doctors reasoned that the A.M.A. was likely to prohibit doctors from taking the training. The group recommended that José wait until Silva had trained a few thousand M.D.s. Then they could go before the A.M.A. with more backing. The decision turned out to be a wise one, because individual doctors who used the Silva Method in their practice found themselves harassed by hospitals and local boards.

One Pennsylvania doctor was so effective at healing through clairvoyance that an insurance company became interested. This doctor convinced the insurance company representative to join him in approaching his hospital board about arranging a hospital staff Silva training.

As a result of that meeting, the doctor was prohibited from practicing in the hospital, and soon afterward another hospital barred him from practicing there. Finally, he received a letter from the state board saying that if he did not promise—in writing—to stop using clairvoyance, the medical board would not renew his license to practice medicine.

Another hospital experience took place in Milwaukee. José was invited to a meeting there by a hospital director. A surgeon welcomed José, saying that he was the one who arranged the meeting. To those gathered, the surgeon said, "To begin, I want to relate an experience I had with a patient. This woman had to have major surgery. We set a date for the following month, and in the interim she took the Silva training. When the time came for the surgery, she told me about the training and assured me that everything would be all right, that there would be no pain, and that she would heal faster than normal. She also told me she would control her bleeding.

"I said to myself, 'This woman is hallucinating. How, when she is under anesthesia, can she control her bleeding?' But, indeed, she came through the operation with flying colors. She healed very fast and never required painkillers. And from the beginning her bleeding was controlled. She only bled the necessary minimal amount.

"As a surgeon, I have never seen a patient respond in this manner, so I personally am very eager to learn what this mind training is all about. It could be of great value in the medical field."

The audience appeared impressed, and the good doctor should have quit while he was ahead. But then he added, "Can you imagine what it would be like if everybody in this hospital took such training? I for one would like to see if it is possible to train everybody here, including myself, since I would like to learn to do for myself what this patient did for herself. Wouldn't it be great if we could train all the hospital personnel?"

José squirmed in his seat. The doctors and nurses looked at each other. The board of directors sat grimly silent. José thought, "There goes another one." The meeting was over. "Another one" had indeed gone. José never heard from this surgeon again.

José didn't have to guess what happened to him. A researcher or practitioner who steps outside of the accepted boundaries of science as defined by the insiders is hardly ever received by the fraternity with open arms. He or she is usually abruptly rejected and thrust further outside than ever.

One day, José made a decision to confront the scientific fraternity directly. He selected sixty of the leading research scientists in the field of brain and mind research and invited them to Houston, all expenses paid, for a three-day weekend, including airfare, hotel, and meals.

Forty accepted. Twenty refused. The refusals were either attributed to prior commitments or prior bias. The latter claimed that they did not want to have anything to do with Silva ("Please remove my name from your mailing list.") Most of these were from the East, and many of these were or had been connected with Dr. J. B. Rhine of Duke University, who opposed José's work.

The forty who accepted were distinguished researchers from medical clinics, hospitals, universities, and foundations. Several were educators and scientists already connected with the Silva organization.

The opening session was a Friday night dinner. All day Saturday was devoted to a review of the Silva work and the potential it offered to scientific research for the ultimate benefit to humanity. On Sunday, the scientists were treated to a tour of the NASA facilities.

In assessing the weekend, José was satisfied that new friends had been made — although how many and how permanently no one could say. He had done what had to be done to replace ignorance with knowledge. But his effort was a proverbial drop in the bucket. The critics continued to criticize. The skeptics continued to cry fraud. The professionals continued to turn their backs.

But Silva Mind Control continued to grow.

Chapter 11
José Silva Today

The life of José Silva is more than a rags-to-riches story of a poor Mexican-American youth in Laredo; more, too, than a story of a successful lay researcher without any schooling or academic degrees; and more than a story of his triumphs in helping millions to awaken the genius within.

This is a story of a family man. Not just a play-with-the-children-on-Sunday family man, but a family man who feels a oneness with his blood relations and who applies the word *family* to his business associates, the millions of Silva graduates, and to humanity itself.

Silva Mind Control International, Inc., remains today a family-owned, family-run organization. It is not an example of nepotism, but one of devotion.

When José travels to a distant city to provide graduates with advanced training, his sessions are well attended and can gross up in the five figures. But he does not pocket his portion. Eighty percent of it goes into the corporation account, where it is shared by the extended family.

In examining José's personal life, one is taken by the fact that this man lives what he teaches. For example, José teaches that unicameral, or single-hemisphere, thinking is eccentric thinking, but that bicameral thinking—in which both hemispheres are used—is centered thinking. Once trained with the Silva Method, a person is able to use both hemispheres of the mind on an everyday basis. Let's look at just one characteristic of bicameral thinking. The left brain tends to be drawn to detail, to small things, while the right brain looks for the whole picture. José's life is a balance of both predilections. He could be asking Paula if she needed anything from the market in one breath and, in the next breath, discussing with his brother Juan the meditative aspects of classes in India.

Of the apparent dualism in the two perspectives and its resolution, José remarks, "Often, small details do not get the attention

they deserve. Big things are nothing more than the accumula-
tion of small things. It stands to reason, then, that small details
make big things happen. The man who does small things well,
regardless of their apparent unimportance, will do big things well.
Making it a habit to do small things well—day in and day out,
regardless of how insignificant they may seem—will eventually
program us to do big things well."

Another attribute of right-brain thinking is unity. This con-
trasts with the left brain's preference for dichotomy. Many
writers advise that executives leave their business in the office,
suggesting that taking it home involves stress. But José is never
separated from his work, and his family is quite comfortable with
his sudden phone calls or unexpected flashes of insight.

"Better call off that picnic outing for today."

"Why?"

"I have a hunch."

And it rains.

When his son Antonio was called for service in Vietnam, in
September 1966, this was both a family *and* a Mind Control matter. Antonio and José decided that programming was needed
to help prepare the boy for the dangers encountered in warfare.
They set a date to begin, and when that day arrived, a whole
group of young men joined Antonio for the training—men who
had volunteered with Antonio to enter the service.

The group learned to awaken automatically should danger approach, to stop pain in themselves and others, and to halt bleeding in themselves and in others. The Three-Fingers Technique,
where the tips of the thumb, index finger, and middle finger
are put together in a signal to the mind to work at a deeper level
of awareness and to trigger already established programs, was
specially adapted for warfare, making it possible for the soldier
to keep his hand free to form a fist, fire a rifle, or use some other
weapon requiring the full use of all of the fingers and both hands.
José changed the technique so that Antonio and his buddies
could fold the little finger of either hand to touch the palm in
order to trigger alpha level and previously programmed responses
while still maintaining optimum alertness.

Every single one of the specially trained youngsters returned safely from battle action . . . with many stories to tell. In fact, other soldiers had become aware that there was something special about Antonio's group in Vietnam and would follow its men around for advice and safety.

Once, Antonio's patrol was ambushed. He was riding in an armored personnel carrier and firing a 50-caliber machine gun when a rocket hit the side of his vehicle. Instead of exploding on impact, the rocket penetrated both sides ending as a dud at a distance. But the jolt slammed the machine gun handle into Antonio's chest, causing a temporary paralysis of the left arm. The driver took over manning the machine gun, and Antonio drove the vehicle back to safety, one-handed. By the time he arrived at the hospital, his arm was back to normal.

Every so often, José meets one of the boys he trained for the Vietnam venture. They invariably raise an arm with the little finger folded touching their palm and say, "Hi, Mr. Silva."

José regrets that he had not perfected his method before World War II, in time to train his brothers and sisters by his mother's second marriage. Perhaps his brother Richard would not have lost his life at Iwo Jima if he had had access to this valuable tool.

A fairly recent family photograph shows José and Paula with their ten children. Another family photograph, taken at the same time, shows José and Paula with not only the ten children but also the in-laws and grandchildren. There are thirty-seven people in this picture—truly an "extended" family!

In 1975, José teamed up with a New York City educator to write his first book, with Philip Miele, entitled *The Silva Mind Control Method.** This book was a success and has remained on book trade shelves for the last fifteen years. It was at about this time that I met José. I soon wrote three books in as many years with José.****

*New York: Pocket Books, 1976.
***The Silva Mind Control Method for Business Managers* (New York: Pocket Books, 1987); *The Silva Mind Control Method for Getting Help From Your Other Side* (New York: Pocket Books, 1989); *You the Healer* (Tiburon, California: H J Kramer, 1989).

Travel takes up a large segment of José's personal life. He is motivated less by the opportunities to see new sights, taste new foods, and experience new cultures than by the opportunity to accelerate the spread of the Silva Method to more millions.

Because the demand on José to travel all over the world is so great, he treasures the days at home with Paula, who prefers to stay in Laredo. Now that he is seventy-six, his family makes a concerted effort to see that someone always travels with him. But this is their idea, not his, and recently when a son had to cancel plans to accompany José to California and no last-minute substitute was available, José went on his own, undaunted. He not only gave a seminar on that trip but spent a grueling day autographing books and being interviewed.

At the risk of "telling tales out of school," I can report that I was once driving José around to see the sights of Honolulu—the capitol building with its volcano motif and the only royal palace in the United States—when I heard quiet snoring and noticed his head on his chest. I decided to drive back to Waikiki. On the way back, I could not help but notice a tall bikini-clad blonde walking on the sidewalk in high heels. Just then the snoring stopped, and José's head came up. "Look at that," he said; a second later, he was snoring again.

José remains physically agile and active as well as mentally sharp and perceptive as he enters his late seventies. White-haired and bespectacled, his teeth, muscle tone, and energy belie his years, and his voice still has the ring of youth. He still enjoys lecturing and experimenting with the Silva biofeedback equipment—the skin galvanic reactors, the stimulators, and the EEGs. Further, he still loves burning the midnight oil to read the latest biographies, scientific books, and technical articles on brain/mind functioning. He considers fiction a waste of time. He enjoys encouraging people to use more of their minds to solve problems and to improve the world.

José has received many honors: He has been given several honorary degrees, named honorary ambassador-at-large by the governor of Guam, and awarded several patents. He heads a number of corporations and holds the key to the city of Laredo. Regarding all these achievements, he remains modest.

Despite the many injustices of the press with respect to his work, José never refuses an invitation to be interviewed for newspapers, radio, or television. It is always his hope that his right-brain enlightenment will penetrate the left-brain bias of the interviewer or editor.

On one occasion, José was invited to participate in a television show in New York along with a man who had been a rabid critic in the past. José accepted, but on one condition: that he not be insulted, for if he was, he would fight back. It was so agreed.

The television show had been proceeding smoothly when the critic interjected, "I understand that you teach people clairvoyance and that you can detect health problems in people, even at a distance."

"Yes, that is so," answered José.

"Well, I just happen to have a case described on a piece of paper in my pocket right now. I want you to tell me what is wrong with this person."

"You have been our worst critic," replied José. "You have called us unscientific. And here you want me to relax and work a case on television. Is this a scientific setting? These things are done scientifically in a laboratory. I thought you were a scientist!" It was color television, and the camera caught the critic's face turning many colors. In the remaining minutes of the program, he failed to recover his poise.

José and Paula live in a modest ranch house just a few footsteps from Silva Headquarters, still in the same building where he began his initial activities in 1962. In a nearby building, a small printing plant turns out manuals, directives, brochures, and newsletters. Here, too, the fifty employees in the headquarters compound assemble biofeedback equipment.

José is constantly on the move among the three buildings, and the switchboard operators have difficulty keeping up with him.

One might find him in the equipment area using the Silva Stimulator. Through two metal grips, microsecond bursts of electricity are sent up through the user's arms.

"This builds muscles," he would explain. "It stimulates the circulation and nervous systems. I use it every day."

A few minutes later, he might be consulting with his brother
Juan on a problem in some foreign country or going over domestic statistics with Alejandro González, Jr., his senior vice president and administrator. Or he might be reviewing the next
edition of the Silva Method newsletter with communications
specialist Ed Bernd, Jr. Then he might drive his Rolls Royce,
the gift of a grateful graduate, to the airport to meet his daughter Laura, on her way back from a seminar. Next he might lunch
with Paula and perhaps take a nap, with more work at headquarters in the afternoon, punctuated by long-distance calls from
all over the world and an occasional appointment with a visiting lecturer.

An ordinary day in the life of an extraordinary man at the
center of a worldwide network—of superminds!

Chapter 12
José Silva's Spiritual Beliefs

We have already traced José's relationship with Jesus and how a number of "coincidences" has convinced him that he is doing the work that Jesus would have all of us do.

But to get to the essence of José's spiritual beliefs, we need the answers to certain questions.

Suppose we just go ahead and ask him.

Stone: What is life all about?

Silva: I perceive that we have been assigned to this planet by our Creator to perfect creation, to find solutions to existing problems.

Stone: You say you "perceive" it. How did you "perceive" it?

Silva: When you use the left brain to think about such a question, you are drawing on past experiences, which do not help much with such a problem. When, in addition, you use the right brain hemisphere, a more in-depth analysis takes place. You understand things from a larger, you might say universal, perspective.

Stone: Finding solutions to problems — that sounds pretty serious. Aren't we supposed to have any fun?

Silva: It depends on what you mean by "fun." I don't endorse an entire city going on holiday to honor a baseball player whose home runs helped win a pennant. Stores are closed, people parade, bands play. Do we do that for a scientist who makes an important discovery?

Stone: Are you against sports?

Silva: Sports are fine as a means of exercise and keeping fit. But what exercise do the tens of thousands of spectators get? I myself learned boxing, not only to keep myself in good physical condition, but to defend myself if needed.

Stone: What about professional boxing?

Silva: It gives me great sorrow to see a beautiful specimen of a human body, the most wonderful expression of our Creator, being beaten to a pulp, sometimes maimed or paralyzed for life.

Stone: And football?

Silva: Here, too, the risk of damaging the perfect creations of God just for the sport of it does not make sense to me. The first-time observer of football would probably think that the ball used to be round, but so many of these big men falling on it and piling on top of each other caused the ball to become elliptical. The fact that these men who are fighting for the little ball, running back and forth, are paid more than what is paid to scientists who are trying to solve problems of creation and are serving the Creator and not throwing their time away does not make sense. After these players earn more than enough to meet their needs and make it into the Hall of Fame, does that mean that they met with their obligation toward the Creator of correcting the problems of Creation and making this planet a better place to live?

Stone: What about the good side of sports—improving the physical body, setting goals and reaching them?

Silva: That's fine for the participants, especially in the form of physical training programs in the educational system. But I deplore the billions on billions of man hours spent throughout the world in deriving entertainment from sports. Imagine what could be done with this time and money if directed at correcting some of the problems threatening life on this planet.

Stone: Where did we go wrong?

Silva: By not recognizing Rabbi Jesus and the Christ mission. We missed his message—that he came to save us from suffering because of our ignorance in not using what God had given us, a right side to our brain.

Stone: And why has it lasted all these centuries?

Silva: Parents taught left-brain thinking to their children, ignoring right-brain thinking. So this limited conditioning and programming has been passed from generation to generation.

Stone: What can we do about it?

Silva: We need to recall Christ's message and put it into practical use today.

Stone: How would you sum up Christ's message?

Silva: Go to the kingdom within. Become centered and clairvoyant. Thus one becomes prophetic and wise. Once prophetic and wise, mistakes lessen, suffering diminishes. Christ taught

that this was the way to eliminate ignorance and save humanity from suffering.

Stone: You don't hear his message spelled out in that way from
most pulpits.

Silva: I believe that more and more clergy are getting the message. Its time has come. There is a movement on.

Stone: Is the Silva Method part of that movement?

Silva: Once a person activates the right hemisphere and becomes prophetic and wise, that person must help others to
become clairvoyant. This is what I have been doing, and, through
the Silva Method, what hundreds of others have been doing—
training people to become centered in their thinking and wise, to
correct the problem of omission that Christ came here to correct.

Stone: Will humanity ever get back on track?

Silva: Hopefully, our millions of graduates will trigger more
millions to act on Jesus' message. I thank Rabbi Jesus. I ask him
to forgive us for taking two thousand years to understand the
Christ message.

It is apparent that José Silva considers his mission in this life
to further Jesus' mission. This does not mean he considers himself in any way another Jesus. Rather, it means he respects the
inspiration and enlightenment that has come his way and wants
to share it. He has received enough spiritual "signs" of confirmation that he is convinced he is on the right track.

José and the author are not suggesting divine intervention in
the success of the Silva Method. But José believes that a person who solves any kind of a problem is helping the Creator
with creation, since a problem can be defined as anything that
hurts the Creator's creation, including his creatures. So the more
problems you solve, the closer you come to the Creator—that
is, the more you are on the Creator's side. It is only logical, then,
that the Creator is on your side all the more.

José's personal and business life is devoted to solving problems. His colleagues consider him downright stubborn in that
regard. Says one, "He believes in himself. When there's opposition or criticism, he fights that much harder. He never
gives up."

The more problems we cause, the farther we get from the Creator. José and his brother Juan are scrupulously generous and loving in their business relationships.

A coordinator who is not fair in the financial settlement made with a visiting lecturer is given another chance and another and another.

One lecturer who won the President's Cup for the record number of his graduates one year stopped sending Laredo class reports or royalties. Another company would probably have dunned the lecturer for a few months and then revoked his authorization to teach. In this case, the lecturer was considered to be in some temporary financial difficulty, and rather than cause him a problem, the Silva organization exercised patience. That patience finally ran out after two years, and it was decided that the lecturer had misinterpreted Laredo's patience as permissiveness.

"How about one more question, José?"

"Fire away, Bob."

"What do you believe about God?"

"I believe in a hierarchy of intelligence in the universe—that there is a certain level of intelligence assigned to govern the galaxy we call the Milky Way, a higher level to govern a group of galaxies, and the greatest of all intelligences, God, whose domain is the entire universe."

The more we solve problems, José believes, the higher we evolve in this order of intelligence. Eventually, we can become godlike. In other words, we have been created in the image of God. The more centered we become in our thinking, the less destructive and the more creative we become. The image becomes more focused, more as it was created to be.

The process of going to your alpha level, identifying the problem, fixing it in your imagination, and mentally seeing the solution in its place therefore becomes a spiritual act.

If one compares it to prayer, it becomes apparent that such dynamic meditation is more creative than supplication. In fact, if the Creator made us in his image to perfect creation on earth, prayer is like turning the job back to him.

It would seem more appropriate for God to pray to us.

Maybe he has been doing just that for two thousand years. When I was invited to India to lecture on the Silva Method and to teach dynamic meditation, I was challenged by an Indian meditator.

"Dr. Stone, aren't you storming the gates of heaven?"

My reply was perhaps a bit indignant. "Let's storm them. We've been pussyfooting outside them long enough!"

I think José would agree with me—at least in the sense that we were not created to bask in the light of our Creator, but rather to do his work with him. Then and only then, José says, will we change from hurting and killing each other. Instead, we will help each other to convert this planet into a paradise.

If José is frustrated by the inflexibility of scientists, he is even more frustrated by religious leaders whose dogma remains a barrier to change. "It is their holy obligation to come forward and help us get the job done," José insists. "And the sooner, the better."

If religious leaders were to carry the ball—it is really their ball to carry—and if they were to train their congregations to develop the right hemisphere, which is our connection to the spiritual self, educators would be more inclined to follow suit, and education, imbued with clairvoyance, could turn out students with doctorates as young as age fifteen, in José's opinion.

It is not a heavy ball to carry. In the final portion of this book, I describe the procedures of each of the customary four days of the Silva Method training. One cannot give or receive the training from these chapters. But these chapters provide more than the usual introductory lecture given free around the world as a means of clarifying the nature and benefit of the training to enable a decision to be made.

If you read these chapters and feel drawn to the training, two options are open to you:

1. Find out where the nearest training will be held by writing or telephoning Silva Method headquarters in Laredo.*

*Silva Mind Control International, Inc., P.O. Box 2249, Laredo, TX 78044-2249. Phone: (512) 722-6391. FAX: (512) 722-7532.

2. Train yourself by following the forty-day program in *You the Healer* by José Silva and myself and published by the same publisher, H J Kramer, as this book you are reading.

New Age thinking emphasizes that we are not creatures of circumstance but creators of circumstance. What does this mean? It means that you relax and go within. This state is like a reverie. You picture the unwanted condition to identify the problem. You then picture wanted conditions to create the solution.

This is oversimplification, but let's take a look at what is actually happening. This is left-brain world. By definition, it is material. As material, it is the domain of the left brain. So, during most of our waking hours—on the job or off the job—we are largely functioning with only the left side of the brain.

This is like going through life with one arm tied behind your back. Your right brain is more valuable than you think (with your left brain). The reason is that the right brain's domain is not the physical world in which you must survive, but its realm is the cause of that physical world. The cause of the physical world lies in the Creative Realm.

So, when you relax and mentally picture, your relaxation triggers right-brain functioning and what you mentally picture triggers the Creative Realm to produce it.

That does not sound like the Silva Method, does it? It sounds like the Creative Method. It sounds like something we were born to do naturally.

Humanity made a wrong turn somewhere along the way. Maybe it was in the Garden of Eden when Adam and Eve first ate of the fruit of the knowledge of good and evil—such polarity being strictly left brain.

So why do we need a method to get back on track? It takes reprogramming to change behavior. We need to know how to reprogram and possibly even have somebody—like a certified Silva Method lecturer—help us reprogram.

José feels that it was Jesus' mission to get us back on track—to restore the bridge between the material world and the Creative Realm—but that we were not paying attention.

We are still not paying attention. Ten million superminds are but a drop in a five-billion bucket. The prisons and hospitals are still full. Gunfire can still be heard. The life-supporting environment of planet earth is being put more and more at risk.

"How do we apply for help to solve a problem, José?"

"It must be done from a spiritual level of mind, called the Holy Ghost dimension, that is found within every one of us. Once you have learned to enter that dimension, and if you are convinced that there are higher levels of intelligence in the universe, then you program yourself to automatically awaken at night when all conditions are optimum to make contact with a higher level of intelligence. If what you ask for is possible, and doesn't create a problem for somebody somewhere else, higher intelligence will help you solve your problem, usually within three days."

"Are there any ifs, ands, or buts, José?"

"You must have a problem that concerns yourself or others. You must have exhausted all means within your reach to solve it."

José deplores the fact that preachers value Jesus' crucifixion and blood more than they do his message. They talk about the kingdom of heaven as if it were in the hereafter. Jesus was not a public relations man for the hereafter. He came here to help solve problems on earth.

Where is the kingdom of heaven? For the answer, José refers us to the New American Standard Bible, chapter 9, verse 33: "First seek the kingdom of heaven (God) that is within you and function within God's righteousness and everything else will be added unto you."

José is quick to point out that he has no degrees in theology and that he is not licensed to preach in any religious organization. He is also quick to point out that the truth is not limited to scholars and that it was the scholars of that day who said Jesus was in league with the devil and who criticized and condemned him.

The author really has no right to pen this chapter. It should have been written by José himself. Let me atone in part by letting José finish this chapter in words gleaned from his unpublished works:

"Were the seven days of creation the same kind of days we know? Of course not. They were days to the Creator—ages to us, perhaps hundreds of thousands of years in each universal day.

"Jesus understood that the seventh day, the last day of the creation, was the day when God allowed man to take over the task, to finish the job of creating a paradise.

"After all, God is already perfect; humans are not. So humans need to practice solving problems, to learn to be better problem solvers, to learn to be more creative, to learn to be more like the Creator."

Chapter 13
José Silva's Scientific Beliefs

The staff at Laredo appears to be a bit uneasy when José gets bold enough to express his spiritual beliefs — an event that is becoming more and more frequent.

The staff is much more comfortable when he sticks to his scientific research and the physiology and psychology behind the Silva Method. Not that Silva personnel necessarily have different spiritual beliefs from José. They just don't want their chief to become a guru. They prefer to see him as the lay scientist that he is, and the foremost authority on mind training in the world today. Riding a donkey, spreading the gospel? No! Jetting around the world with brain-wave monitoring equipment? Yes!

But there is an anomaly. José's scientific beliefs dovetail with his spiritual beliefs. It is hard to tell where one set of beliefs leaves off and the other begins. It is as if the no-man's-land that has traditionally existed between science and religion has shrunk. José sees a field of intelligence, albeit in hierarchies of intensity, filling all space — by whatever name.

A fringe group of scientists has slowly come around to proposing this same concept. To classical scientists, this group constitutes the lunatic fringe. But it was ever thus. Scientists appear to go through three stages. First they say, "You're crazy!" Then they say, "We'll look into it." Finally they say, "We've known it all along."

The fringe of scientists that sees space as more than the conventional nothingness is widening. As the shift from Newtonian to Einsteinian physics accelerates, their numbers are increasing. Quantum physics is physics catching up to José Silva, the nonscholar, the uneducated. As Fritjof Capra illustrated in *The Tao of Physics,** it is virtually impossible to distinguish the findings of researchers in the new physics from the beliefs of Chinese philosophers millennia ago.

*New York: Bantam, 1977.

Space is somethingness.

Detecting that a person thousands of miles away has gallstones, imagining crushing those gallstones with your fingers, seeing them dissolve, and then getting feedback that the person is free of the gallstones — which is an everyday accomplishment by Silva trainees — is impossible to Newton but fits into Einstein's possibilities as consciousness comes to be recognized as energy, and the human body is recognized as the effect with energy as its cause.

José may not use accepted scientific terms in his own explanation to trainees, but the results are the same. The trainees begin to understand that their mental images are creative, that there is no time and no space in the Creative Realm, and that they can create perfection in the "soul mold," which is the term he gives to the energy body that forms the physical body.

Because his initial interest in mind training was inspired by the psychiatric tests he received on entering the army and the way they paralleled the electronic testing he had become familiar with through his practice of radio repair, José was quick to see the computerlike aspect of the human brain.

By slowing the brain waves, which brought both halves of the brain into balance, that computer could be fed data or programmed. For many of the first of his twenty-two years of research, José's scientific inquiry was devoted to ways of slowing the brain waves and of programming the mind. Only in the latter years of that research and the early years of the Silva Method launching, did José begin to utilize new findings about the different characteristics of left and right brain functioning and use those findings to explain how the right brain provided our connection to Higher Intelligence.

It was then that the no-man's-land between José's scientific views and his spiritual views disappeared.

The mind was like a personal computer that could be connected to a computer with a larger data bank. This larger computer, this Higher Intelligence, must have wanted its smaller brethren to make more use of it as things went poorly on earth. One scientist — Dr. Rupert Sheldrake, a British botanist — called the connection between data banks a field of intelligence and gave it a name: the morphogenetic field. He hypothesized that there was such a field not only for humans but for rats, for rabbits, for every species. Every test Sheldrake devised—and that others devised at his invitation—confirmed the existence of this shared intelligence. Laboratory mice traversed a maze faster once this task was learned by laboratory mice thousands of miles away. People who knew no Hungarian learned an old Hungarian nursery rhyme faster than another group learned a new one of the same length.

As Jung's concept of the collective unconscious was being replaced by Sheldrake's morphogenetic field, José was making scientists sit up and take notice through conscious control of subconscious bodily functions. As Sheldrake's morphogenetic field theory was joined by Dr. Karl Pribram's and Dr. David Bohm's holographic theory of the mind, in which they see the human brain as containing the whole of the universe, José was teaching the control of mental imaging to create what is pictured. As Dr. Peter Russell was identifying the existence of a global brain that helped regulate the ecology of the planet, José was explaining to trainees how their right hemispheres were their connections to a larger intelligence.

In a Texas medical laboratory engaged in cancer research, white rats were being injected with cancer cells to grow tumors so that those tumors could then be used to test cures for humans. José was asked, "Can you program healthy rats to grow tumors naturally?"

"We do not use our training for hurting any living thing, anytime, for any reason," José replied.

"But think of all the cattle, pigs, chickens, and turkeys butchered every day for the survival of the human species. If we have to kill all the rats in the world to save one human life, we will do it," urged the doctor.

"All right," agreed José, "let's go to the lab."

José programmed the rats to develop tumors naturally. A month later, he was called back to the laboratory to see the successful results. The doctor was quick to acknowledge the impact of this.

"If the mind can do this," he mused, "then the mind can undo it."

José's silence spoke unmistakably. "That's what I've been training people to do, my friend."

"Wait a minute," you say, especially if you are one of those trainees. "I thought we cannot hurt life or create problems with this power?"

José is quick to explain. "We have two kinds of energy: objective, or physical, energy, and subjective, or mental, energy. We can use both kinds of energy in a person's presence. The objective energy can either help or harm. The subjective energy can only help.

"At a distance, we can transmit only subjective energy. Subjective energy is an attractive force—that is, it attracts matter to conform to the perfect pattern that nature intended. Thus, it cannot be used to hurt or harm. However, when I programmed the healthy rats to grow tumors, I used objective energy, programmed in the beta brain-wave state, and was in the immediate environment. There are many negative-energy generators in the environment, creating problems. I became one of them in this case."

Needless to say, since the Silva Method is training in the use of subjective energy, it cannot be used for harm. As further guarantee of this, the trainees repeatedly accept the following programming: "You will never use these levels of the mind to harm any human being; if this be your intention, you will not be able to function within these levels of the mind. You will always use these levels of the mind in a constructive, creative manner for all that is good, honest, pure, clean, and positive."

Problems with objective energy are constantly arising between people. We take away each other's confidence. We impose stress. We sow seeds of fear. The Silva Method uses subjective energy to counteract this.

It is inevitable that José's scientific approach in the training takes on spiritual overtones. Take the fact that he says he gets better results when, during programming for a solution to a problem, he lowers his head as if in prayer. His explanation: "I have observed, while working hundreds of cases, that I have gotten better results when I present the case with my head lowered as in prayer. To me, it seemed that if I did not lower my head, I would not register my tries.

"When I tried, and tried again, and could not solve the problem, only when I had registered my tries—that is, when I tried with my head lowered—would I be entitled to get help from Higher Intelligence. If I tried to solve a case with my head straight up, it did not matter how many times I tried. When I asked for help, I would not get it.

"In straightforward language, it appears that we register our tries on a meter when we try with our heads lowered, and we would not register our tries with our head straight up. Then it seems that when we ask for help, some High Intelligence comes along and, before helping, looks at the meter. If tries have not been registered, we don't get help. If they have, we do get help."

This blending of the scientific and the spiritual became increasingly common in José's presentations. After all, he is a bicameral thinker—with his left-brain input based on the material world's science and his right-brain input based on spirituality of the Creative Realm.

Another typical example occurred when José was the dinner speaker attended by insurance executives of W. Clement Stone's company. After explaining the brain as a biological computer that we can learn to self-program, and explaining its immensity if duplicated by an electronic counterpart, he compared its programming to Christ's training of prophets and wise men and His saying that it was "now at hand."

José then went on to say, "You and I and every human being were born multimillionaires because our Creator gave each and every one of us a biological computer-type brain that functions on an average of twenty-five watts of self-created power. It is very light and portable. We carry it with ease on our shoulders and can program it on the spot.

"The one thing we need to know," he added, "is how to program it. Through our clairvoyant training, we learn how to program our biological computer brain to respond on full automatic, semi-automatic, or direct manual control."

As scientists become exposed to the "miracles" possible through clairvoyant thinking, they quickly fall back on the repeatability concept. If it can be done again and again, under identical conditions, then they have something into which they can sink their scientific teeth.

However, when brain neurons are involved in an experiment, or even other cells of animals and plants, the experiment is "known" to be unreal. Cleve Backster has demonstrated with both plants and human cells that each is aware of laboratory protocol and, when monitored, shows none of the reaction in the lab that it shows when there is spontaneous reality.

José reminded the insurance agents at their dinner that "the complex human brain—the highest masterpiece of our Creator— should not be used for nonsense applications when its purpose is for solving real, existing problems of creation." He explained how the brain neurons know a hypothetical situation from a real one. They will not engage in synthetic problem solving but will solve real problems because that is what they have been programmed to do.

The dinner talk was well received. But one young executive confronted José and said repeatedly, "Guess my name. Guess my name." His face was so close to José's that he was spitting in his face. José backed away, but the spitting face followed him. "As close as we are, I'll bet you cannot guess my name."

"If you have forgotten your name, I'll turn on my multimillion-dollar computer brain right now and get your name for you," José replied.

The man turned around and left.

Comments José on that incident: "I think I know what Christ meant when he said, 'Some have ears and do not hear. Some have eyes and do not see.' I would like to add, with Christ's permission, some have brains and minds but do not understand."

Another obstacle to the classic scientific verification of consciousness-based phenomena is the mind-set of the scientist.

Earlier this century, when scientists were using the aperture test to determine whether light was wave or particle, some scientists got a wave result, while others got a particle result. A determining factor was that each got the result that each expected. Light, having the characteristics of both wave and particle, was being affected by the consciousness of the experimenter.

Scientists who still feel they are objective observers of an experiment dealing with the mind are doomed to frustration. Their own minds are one of the variables in the experiment.

Graduates who recycle the Silva Method training and who sit in on the final case-working session to observe the degree of the new trainees' success have to be reminded not to worry about "misses"—in order not to increase the likelihood of such "misses." "Remember, you are observing geniuses at work" is the author's usual instruction to the old graduates at that point. And the new graduates receive, instead of mental interference, mental support.

Anecdotal reports of benefits from the training are as numerous as the millions of graduates. As a lay scientist, José appreciates the superior value of scientific studies and has encouraged such research into both physiological and psychological benefits.

Dr. J. W. Hahn, in recent Mind Science Foundation studies, has surveyed more than a thousand trainees. Some of the findings of these studies are the following:

Although only 24.2 percent sought health benefits from the use of Mind Control techniques, 49.1 percent reported improved health.

Although only 10.7 percent sought improved sleep without drugs, 34.9 percent reported this as a benefit.

The ability to relax deeply, critical to the reduction of potentially damaging physical tension and psychological stress, was sought by 34.8 percent, obtained by 70.3 percent.

The original purpose of José's research was to discover ways to enhance learning ability. His own children and his neighbors' children were the original subjects and showed marked improvement in their school grades.

Later, scientific testing became possible in a number of schools. It would have been valuable if a standard IQ test could have been used. But such tests are largely left-brain oriented and would not reflect increased right-brain activity, which is one of the major benefits of the Silva training.

Instead, personality tests, published by the Institute for Personality and Ability Testing, were used. For student and adult groups, some of the results of this before-and-after testing, conducted by Dr. George T. DeSau, some in collaboration with Paul Seawell, follow:

High school students showed a strong movement away from the tendency to become upset and toward the qualities of "high ego strength, mature, faces reality, calm."

Adults moved away from patterns indicating "tense, frustrated, driven, overwrought" and toward responses indicating "relaxed, tranquil, unfrustrated, composed."

In testing for social orientation, there was a shift away from "shy, timid, threat sensitive" and toward "spontaneous, socially bold."

Participants who were rated competitive, suspicious, and mistrustful later showed a greater willingness to work with others.

Testing recorded a movement away from "reserved, detached, critical, aloof" and toward "warmhearted, outgoing, participating."

Gloominess and pessimism changed to greater cheerfulness, enthusiasm, and joie de vivre, indicating a newfound freedom from inner turmoil.

Is it any wonder that José's goal goes well beyond ten million?

To end the planet's problems, *everybody* must function with both sides of the brain and become clairvoyant and wise.

Part II
The Silva Method

Chapter 14
The Silva Training:
Day 1

Certainly, no portrait of José Silva would be complete without an inside look at what goes on in the four days of a Silva Method training, the result of José's lifework. In a sense, in reading the training descriptions, you will have taken the course itself. However, because the training is designed to develop the right brain, simply reading the steps will not substitute for attending the four days of classes. You may be more enlightened about the man and his method, but you will not be a clairvoyant.

The four days of the training are each identified by number and name:

1. Mind Control 101, Controlled Relaxation (abbreviated MC101CR)
2. Mind Control 202, General Self-Improvement (MC202GSI)
3. Mind Control 303, Effective Sensory Projection (MC303ESP)
4. Mind Control 404, Applied Effective Sensory Projection (MC404AESP).

The text in Part One has described the free introductory lectures. If you had attended such a lecture, the trainer would have ended with a list of the many benefits of learning to control your mental level, including:

- How to remain calm all the time
- How to get sleep anytime, anywhere, no matter how anxious you might be
- How to awaken without an alarm clock
- How to be alert and energetic anytime, no matter how tired you are
- How to remember thirty items or more with only a few minutes of preparation

- How to turn off a headache (even a migraine) in minutes, without drugs
- How to dream solutions to your problems and execute those solutions
- How to read faster, understand better, recall more, and get better grades, all with less study
- How to meditate anytime, anywhere
- How to get healthier and stay that way
- How to remember dreams and dream solutions
- How to solve problems automatically
- How to stop smoking with ease
- How to lose weight without dieting
- How to concentrate completely, anytime, anywhere
- How to be more successful
- How to restore energy in seconds
- How to improve communication
- How to improve your IQ
- How to be more efficient effortlessly
- How to enhance your self-esteem

Day 1 is about to begin. It is 9 A.M. You have paid your tuition, received a training manual, clipped on your name tag. A large percentage of Silva lecturers are women, so let us assume that the lecturer here is a woman. The lecturer begins by explaining how the training is conducted.

"This is subjective training. As such, it is quite different from what you are probably used to in standard objective training. It is different because there is no need to take notes, no studying, no homework, no tests. The harder you try, the *worse* will be the results, not the better.

"Subjective learning occurs not when you try but when you close your eyes, relax, and listen. During the training, you will be asked to do things mentally—either to say or picture something. That's when subjective learning takes place.

"Your manual is not really a study tool but more a security blanket," the lecturer continues. "It reassures you that if you should ever need to remind yourself of some Silva procedure, you'll be able to look it up."

Next comes an explanation of how the training works. "First, I lecture, as I am doing now. Next, I explain the content of the conditioning cycle to be read for relaxation and programming. Then I read the cycle to you while you relax. After the cycle, we discuss it if necessary." The conditioning cycle *is* the training. It is a reading containing relaxing instructions plus affirmations and imaging exercises.

The lecturer turns her attention to the concept of relaxation and the slowing of the brain-wave frequency as illustrated on the Scale of Brain Evolution chart (see page 11).

"We move through the alpha level—seven to fourteen brain waves per second—twice daily, on our way to sleep at night and as we awaken in the morning. So the alpha level is nothing strange for any of us. What you will be learning here is to stay there for a while."

The trainer then reviews the ground to be covered this first day, which will include six conditioning cycles:

1. A brief test of cooperation and an introduction to relaxation.
2. Deepening of the relaxation and beginning the process of programming with beneficial statements and illness-prevention.
3. A long relaxation, in which the different stages of relaxation are assigned numbers for their better control; the introduction of programming to project sensing faculties anywhere.
4. A short relaxation, with three deep breaths, numbered three, two, and one, automatically bringing you to the alpha level.
5. The introduction of three formula-type techniques to produce specific benefits—Sleep Control, to take you at will into normal, natural, healthy sleep without the use of drugs; Awake Control, to enable you to wake up naturally without an alarm clock; and Stay Awake Control—to end drowsiness whenever so desired.
6. Dream Control and Headache Control, to generate, remember, and understand dreams for problem solving and to end tension and migraine headaches.

The lecturer begins to describe the first conditioning cycle. "I'll ask you to raise first your left hand, then your right, and to keep them raised until I ask you to put it down. Then I will have you close your eyes for half a minute or so, to get accustomed to sitting with your eyes closed in a room full of strangers, something we do not do every day. When you open your eyes, I'll remind you that with eyes closed you are at a lower brain-wave frequency. By keeping your eyes closed during these conditioning cycles, you can learn to function at the alpha frequency of the brain. Thus, closing the eyes becomes a simple Silva Method Technique to learn to function mentally at alpha. At the end of the training, however, you will be able to function at alpha with your eyes open whenever necessary."

Next comes the second part of this conditioning cycle. The instructor will read a number of steps to relaxation and the first programming statement.

"The difference between genius mentality and lay mentality is that geniuses use more of their minds and use them in a special manner. You are now learning to use more of your mind and to use it in a special manner.

"This statement is programming you to be a genius, but it's carefully framed to be believable. Your critical thinking faculty might reject as illogical the possibility of your being programmed to be a genius. José Silva spent long years of research to develop the training, using his own children as subjects. He paid particular attention to the language of the statements he used with them. The children became geniuses and clairvoyants," she concludes, "and so will you."

She then describes the final part of the conditioning cycle — reviewing the process of ending by counting up from one to five.

Next, the instructor tests the participants for cooperation. "This, of course, is completely voluntary. All who want to learn our techniques of mind control raise your left hands. Don't lower your hands until I say so. Now, everybody lower your hand."

Less than five minutes later, she ends the cycle by counting from one to five and snapping her fingers. "Eyes open, wide awake, feeling fine and in perfect health, feeling better than before."

A little over an hour may have passed since the start of this first day, and it is time for the first of several coffee breaks. Some lecturers ask the students to introduce themselves before the break, giving their names and, if they wish, their occupations and identifying themselves as new students or returning graduates.

After a short break, the trainer commences by explaining the importance of following instructions. "Being successful in this training requires only that you follow instructions. If you follow instructions, you will succeed. As an example, there was a man who had a mouse in his house. He had a trap but no cheese, so he cut out a color photo of a wedge of cheese from an ad in a slick magazine and used that picture of cheese to bait the trap that night. In the morning, he found in the trap a picture of a mouse. The moral of the joke? Put the real thing into these exercises and get the real thing out."

The instructor begins the second conditioning cycle by first reviewing the cycle's content (called preconditioning), then doing the cycle, and finally discussing it. The second cycle includes programming for good health. I'll sum up the usual course of the discussion in a simple question-and-answer format:

Question: When you said we will learn not to get certain specific diseases, such as arthritis, diabetes, cancer, why does the cycle pick those particular diseases?

Answer: These are the diseases we hear most about and therefore the ones that our environment is programming us to get. Therefore, they are the ones we learn most quickly to get.

Question: Why isn't AIDS mentioned?

Answer: You already know how to avoid getting AIDS.

Question: I thought this training was similar to hypnotism. But you read, "You may accept or reject anything I say." That doesn't sound like hypnotism.

Answer: You're right. It doesn't sound like hypnotism because it *isn't* hypnotism. In fact, it's just the opposite. If it were hypnotism, the trainer would control you. Instead, you control yourself at a deeper level than before.

After an hour lunch break, the class returns for four more conditioning cycles. A long relaxation, coming as it does after lunch, removes all doubt more students that they will be able to relax. Some even trespass on the edge of sleep.

Next, a shorter version of this long relaxation programs a sort of conditioning reflex. The trainer guides the class in taking three deep breaths, mentally repeating the number "three" three times on the first breath, "two" three times on the second, and "one" three times on the third. This formula produces the same deep state of relaxation that the long cycles have done.

At this point, the trainer pauses to congratulate the class.

"You have joined the millions who are in control of the alpha level. You can now use it for benefits."

The final two conditioning cycles program participants with simple procedures or formula-type techniques that provide special benefits. The first cycle provides these techniques:

Sleep Control—a simple imaginary chalkboard procedure that brings on normal, natural, healthy sleep. In this procedure, you visualize writing numbers within a circle and then erasing them on a descending scale.

Awake Control—setting the hands of an imaginary clock in order to awaken you automatically.

Stay Awake Control—a simple command to give yourself at the alpha level to program you for renewed energy.

In the final conditioning cycle of the day, the participants learn two more formula-type techniques:

Dream Control—in three steps: to remember a single dream, to remember all of your dreams, and to order a dream to solve a specific problem.

Headache Control—a simple command to give yourself at the alpha level to end the discomfort of a tension-type headache; the technique is administered three times five minutes apart for a single migraine headache.

With this final cycle, the first day of training ends.

Chapter 15
The Silva Training:
Day 2

The instructor begins by reviewing the ground to be covered in this second day of training. "First, we will locate the Mental Screen—giving a name to the mental area where we do our mental picturing—and we will practice the use of it with a memory system that uses mental pictures. The second of today's six conditioning cycles will be to program the Three-Fingers Technique, another way to improve memory by increasing concentration and recall. Then we will create a Mirror of the Mind to use in problem solving. In our fourth conditioning cycle, we will learn how to create a numbness in our hand and pass this on to any pained area. After pain control, we will program another problem-solving formula-type technique called the Glass-of-Water Technique. We'll end with Habit Control, a means of ridding ourselves of unwanted behavior without constantly exerting willpower and effort.

"We will start this morning by locating the Mental Screen. But first are there any questions?"

Perhaps you would like to have confirmation that you are really going to alpha. "Yes," you say. "How do I know I am really relaxing and going to alpha?"

"By the results," the instructor replies quickly. "If your programming does not produce the results you want, you are probably not at alpha. If you *do* successfully attain the result for which you programmed, you were at alpha. But there's another, more empirical, way of confirming your alpha level." She holds up a small gadget. "This is a biofeedback device to test whether you are really relaxing. A lot of good things happen when you relax—muscle tension eases, pulse slows, blood pressure normalizes. This device measures skin galvanic reaction—how the electrical conductivity of your skin drops as you relax. It is part of the lie detector otherwise known as the polygraph."

Suppose she chooses you as a subject to demonstrate the device. You hesitate. How are you going to relax in front of a roomful of people? You sit at the trainer's desk. She wraps the cloth electrodes around two of your fingers and turns on a switch.

"The beeping noise you hear indicates how much electricity is flowing in the circuit. This student isn't relaxed now. In fact, he is probably somewhat tense sitting up here in front of you, so the beep will be fast. As he relaxes and his skin moisture diminishes, the beeps will slow down." She adjusts the beeps to medium rapid and instructs you to relax. "Close your eyes and take those three deep breaths, mentally repeating three, three, three; two, two, two; one, one, one."

When you take the third breath, there is a distinct slowing down of the beeper. Fantastic! Then the beeps speed up again.

"You got excited when it slowed down, so it speeded up. Deepen your relaxation by counting backward from 10 to 1."

Even before you reach the count of 1, the frequency of the beeps has slowed to half. "End your relaxation by counting up from 1 to 5, opening your eyes, and feeling wide awake."

As you count up, the beeper speeds up. When you open your eyes, it is racing.

With the class more confident than ever as to the effectiveness of the training to induce relaxation, the instructor proceeds.

"Yesterday, we gained control of our relaxation. Now we gain control of our visualization and imagination. That completes the two-part formula for changing your life: relax and picture. We use two words for the picturing, *visualize* and *imagine*, because you can *visualize* something you've seen before, but if you've never seen it, you have to *imagine* it.

"For both kinds of picturing, we use the Mental Screen—an internal image of a screen located about twenty degrees above the horizontal plane of sight." She extends her arm out to the side, slightly raised, to indicate the twenty-degree angle. "The twenty degrees means that you must look upward to see an answer on the screen.

"By moving the eyes up in this way, we trigger the brain to sense the answer directly. And in the process we trigger more alpha brain waves. José found that by doing our mental picturing as if there were a screen in that precise position, we would trigger more right-brain activity and be more creative."

The instructor moves on to introduce the Bruno Furst memory system, using as an example of something to be remembered a hypothetical shopping list. Someone suggests shoelaces as the first object on the list. "The first Bruno Furst memory peg picture is a glass of tea, so we must make a mental picture on our Mental Screen that combines the glass of tea and the shoelaces draped over the glass. Then, when we get to the shopping center and picture the first memory peg—a glass of tea—there are the shoelaces on the glass."

She goes over the first ten memory pegs, asking the class to call out items for the shopping list—for example, oranges, a quart of oil, toilet paper, a book, a broom—and suggestions for ways to combine the memory-peg picture with the object.

After this, the instructor leads the class through the conditioning cycle, initially covering the same ground as that covered yesterday. The students take three deep breaths, mentally repeating the numbers three, two, and one three times each. They deepen their relaxation by counting backward from 10 to 1, relaxing their eyelids, and spending a few seconds in some favorite place of relaxation.

You accept the genius statement, beneficial statements such as "Positive thoughts bring me benefits and advantages I desire," and a protective statement about accepting or rejecting what is said: "You are always in control." Now the instructor guides you in making health statements, affirming that you will not learn to get the diseases named and that you "will never learn to develop physical or mental dependence on drugs or alcohol."

The class is assigned a practice session using the Mental Screen, Furst memory system, and the shopping list the class members have come up with.

"The first memory peg is a glass of tea, and the first object is shoe strings. Now associate the two and make some strange or humorous picture that gets your attention." She pauses. You see the laces soggy in the tea.

"The second memory peg is Noah, a man with a white beard.

The object is an orange." You see Noah eating the orange and the juice discoloring his beard.

Picture after picture follows, until thirty are complete. When the conditioning cycle is over, the instructor says, "Okay, class, if I tell you the first memory peg is a glass of tea, you will tell me that the first object is . . . "

The class roars, "Shoelaces!" You come up with object after object as she calls out the memory peg, adding your voice to that of the class. Halfway along, you are suddenly silent. But then you begin to remember again right up until the thirtieth object. You realize that while you were wondering about the system's use for you, you were not making the pictures and that is why you missed those few.

"Remarkable," says the teacher. "How did you remember thirty objects in just two minutes of fun? I'll tell you how. You used the right hemisphere of the brain. Take notice, left brains. You've been suppressing the right brain's input. Left brains, you must respect the ability of your partner, the right brain."

The class generally feels that it performed mentally in a way that the students hadn't thought possible. The use of the right brain encourages them all to go on. The class seems more of a group working together, and the work itself has taken on the feel of a process.

After a short break, the lecturer talks about another way to trigger more alpha brain rhythms. She holds up her hand with her thumb and next two fingers held tightly together. "We're going to create a conditioned reflex," she explains. "Do you remember how Pavlov discovered the conditioned reflex by ringing a bell every time he fed his dogs? Soon, whenever he rang the bell, the dogs would salivate. Well, we are not going to ring bells here and we are not going to salivate, but we are going to program ourselves to return to the alpha level whenever we put these three fingers together.

"In this conditioning cycle, we will program ourselves to have better recall of a lesson read or a lecture heard by using this, the Three-Finger Technique, to return us to alpha. Remember, though, that this is not the only use of this technique. For instance, if you find yourself in a fearful situation, or if you lose your temper, you can use the Three-Finger Technique to remain calm, unafraid, and in full control of your emotions."

After lunch, in the next conditioning cycle, you are guided in creating a mirror. The lecturer explains that this mirror has the capacity to reflect a small scene or a large scene and has a frame that can change color. A blue frame will be used to denote a problem or an unwanted situation. A white frame will be used to denote the solution or a goal reached.

"Whenever you need to use this mirror, called the Mirror of the Mind, to solve a problem or reach a goal, go to your level. See the problem in the blue-framed mirror. Then erase the problem image, move the mirror a bit to the left, toward the future, and see the solution or the goal reached."

"But how can you see the solution in the white-framed mirror if you don't know what it is?"

"In that case, you would not choose the Mirror of the Mind. Rather, you would use the Glass-of-Water Technique, which we will program later this afternoon."

The instructor now prepares to give the class time to solve a problem using this technique. "Start deciding now what personal problem you would like to solve. If you can't think of any, I'll give you one of mine.

"Once you use this technique to solve a particular problem, you will never go back to the blue-framed mirror. Whenever you think of the project you have been treating—note that I do not call it a problem anymore—you will think of it as the solution and see it in the white-framed mirror. This changes the polarity of your thinking. It is typical for left-brained thinkers to sit in a comfortable chair, relax, and daydream about their problems—a habit that does nothing but reinforce them. When you relax and picture, which you do when you visualize your problems, you create. And who needs to create problems? So, we change the polarity of our thinking and instead of creating problems, we create solutions."

Imagine for the moment that your lease is up next month. You decide to use the Mirror of the Mind to solve that problem. Under the guidance of the instructor, you see your apartment in the blue-framed mirror with a calendar on the wall showing this month. You erase that image, change the color of the frame to white, move the Mirror of the Mind slightly, and see a beautiful apartment with a calendar on the wall showing the *next* month.

In the next conditioning cycle, the trainer teaches you to use your hand to go to level in what is called Hand Levitation. In this adaptation of a tool drawn from self-hypnosis, you use your hand to create a numbness that can then be transferred to a pained area.

The lecturer asks class members to drop their hands into an imaginary bucket of ice water and to think about a time when their hands were actually dipped in ice water. Perhaps you remember a picnic when you extracted bottles of soda from a cooler filled with ice cubes. You imagine your hand numb with the cold. In a few seconds, the trainer asks you to test the skin by pinching it with the other hand. The hand is indeed numb.

After the conclusion of the cycle and while the lecturer is explaining how to use your numb hand to relieve pain, you find yourself gazing at a student of the opposite sex two rows in front of you. You close your eyes, take three deep breaths, mentally repeating the numbers three, three, three; two, two, two; one, one, one. Then you picture that student. "My friend," you say mentally, "wouldn't it be nice for you and me if we could chat together. We would both be enriched." You count yourself up.

The lecturer goes on to explain how to use the Glass-of-Water Technique for problem solving. To acquire necessary information or guidance, you merely drink half a glass of water before climbing into bed, close your eyes, turn them slightly upward, and say mentally, "This is all I have to do to solve the problem I have in mind."

The information you need may come in a dream that night. If it does not, finish the glass of water on arising in the same way. The answer will come, the lecturer assures you. Why? Because you are seventy to eighty percent water and the water is programmed to assist human intelligence.

"The Glass-of-Water Technique is useful in other ways as well," the lecturer reminds the class. "It is helpful when you have a decision to make, when you need to find a lost object, or when you need to understand a situation better."

The last conditioning cycle is called Habit Control.

It has been a day full of benefits. You will have five full days before the next session to put some of these formula-type techniques to work.

The lecturer ends the day with a cheery, "Have a great week!"

You have more than a sneaking suspicion it will be.

Chapter 16
The Silva Training:
Day 3

"It's a fact. It happened." You're talking to a few students, who, like yourself, arrived a few minutes early for the third training day. It is now Saturday of the following weekend. "As my problem for the Mirror of the Mind last Sunday, I grappled with my apartment problem just as the instructor suggested. My lease is up, but on Wednesday, a friend in the same building told me he's relocating to another city and his apartment had become available. Of course, I grabbed it. What a coincidence!"

José Silva defines a coincidence as an instance in which "Higher Intelligence has entered the picture but has not signed his name."

"This morning," announces the instructor at the start of Day 3, "we shift gears. If you prefer a sailing metaphor, we go off on a new tack. Whereas last weekend was full of ways to attain benefits, this weekend is focused on mental work. When it is over, the benefits of the work will exceed all those of last weekend.

"Last weekend, we programmed many ways of using the alpha level. We activated more of our minds to go to work for us and learned how to program our minds just as we do a computer. But even though we are now able to use more of our minds than before, part of it is at a disadvantage.

"The right hemisphere has not been educated. It has hardly been used. It has not acquired a storehouse of reference points as the left brain has. All the sights, sounds, smells, tastes, and touches you have experienced since the day you were born are left-brain points of references. The right brain is a virtual wasteland — there are no signposts there, no familiar memories, no points of reference, and when you begin to explore it you get lost. Today and tomorrow morning, we are going to change all that. We are going to supply the right brain with all the advantages of the left brain."

The instructor points to two lists on the chalkboard, one headed "left," the other "right."

Left Brain	Right Brain
External Environment	Internal Environment
Objective	Subjective
Active	Passive
Body Motion	Body Language
Logic	Feeling
Linear	Spatial
Speech, 3 Rs	Music, Art
Detail	Whole Picture
Polarity	Unity

She leaves the chalkboard and walks to where the front row starts. It makes you feel that she wants to be eye to eye with you because she has something important to confide.

"Notice that the last item on the left-brain list is the same as the first. The external environment, which is the physical world, is a polarity. Every atom is a polarity—positive nucleus, negative electrons. If you smash the atom, you get energy. Oneness. One comes before two. So our right brain is attuned to the cause, our left to the effect. Translate this, and it means you and I are a bridge from the Creative Realm—right brain—to the created—left brain."

She points to a man in the front row. "What's the weak side of this bridge?"

"Right-brain side," he replies quickly.

"Correct. We are not well connected to the source of our being, the Creative Realm. We are left-brain thinkers, able to deal fairly well with the material world—with matter, time, and space. But activate the right brain and you add to these abilities that of transcending matter, time, and space in order to think as creators, clairvoyants, psychics, and seers. With the right brain activated, we can solve insoluble problems, know things we have no rational way of knowing. And we can tap into Higher Intelligence."

She walks back to her desk, picks up a large picture, and holds it up. It is an artist's drawing of a man working at his personal computer. A cable connects it to something that fills the whole sky above him. "If you have a computer, you know that you can tap into larger data banks, like library systems, through the phone lines. Similarly, by activating the right side of your mental computer, you can tap into Higher Intelligence, like the Big Computer in the Sky.

"To put it another way, educating the right brain enables us to become psychic, or, if you prefer, intuitive. With this power enhanced, we can depend on our intuition, our ability to guess right."

The first step in educating the right brain is establishing right brain points of reference. The trainer asks the class to enter alpha level, visualize their homes, and scan the outside. You mentally enter your home and go to the living room. You stand in the center of the room, facing the south wall. You scan the wall as you did the outside of the house, top to bottom, left to right, a little lower each time. Then you imagine you are close to the wall, touching. Following the instructions, you mentally project yourself inside the wall, testing for the amount and color of light inside the wall, the temperature, the odor, and finally, by actually making a fist and knocking on the inside of the wall, its solidity as judged by reflected sound. At the count of three and a snap of the instructor's fingers, you are outside the wall and in the center of your living room, facing that wall. The instructor then asks you to change the color of the wall to black, then to red, then to green, then to blue, then to violet, and then back to its normal color and then to black.

Next, you are asked to place some things in front of the black wall in quick succession—a chair, a watermelon, a lemon, an orange, three bananas, three carrots, and finally a fresh, crisp head of lettuce. You examine each of the foods first at a distance, then closer, where you are asked to imagine their odor and taste.

This conditioning cycle may seem endless to you, and you are relieved to hear the instructor say, "Four, five, eyes open, wide awake, feeling fine and in perfect health, feeling better than before."

Why are points of reference necessary; you can understand street signs, maps, tastes, smells, touch, sights, sounds. But this?

During the break, you are asked to examine four small solid metal cylinders—copper, brass, stainless steel, and lead—holding each at arms length, bringing it closer, touching your forehead, and then extending your arm again. After the break, you are told you will repeat this motion in the conditioning cycle, mentally projecting into each metal in order to make the same four tests you made inside the wall as to light, temperature, odor, and solidity.

The instructor explains: "Remember, you will be projecting mentally, not physically. You may be wondering how much space you need to project into these objects mentally—an inch or perhaps a couple of feet? To eliminate the question, we have a technique to make anything bigger and brighter. Simply snap the fingers of your right hand. To restore an object to its original size, snap the fingers of your left hand. Always expect the change to take place."

Once the conditioning cycle has begun, you snap the fingers of your right hand to make the metal object much larger. You hear other fingers snapping around the room.

After lunch, the lecturer explains how subjective points of reference will continue to be programmed in the order of the evolution of matter. "We have already set up right-brain points of reference for metals. Inanimate objects are the least complicated when it comes to programming. Next come plants." She holds up some leaves. "At this point, we will project into these leaves. Projecting into animals is the next most complicated step. I'll ask you to project into a cat or dog you are familiar with, and after that you'll be ready to program points of reference on the human level in order to solve human problems and make this a better world to live in."

The instructor distributes the leaves, a small one and a large one to each student, asking the class to go through the same arm movements with each leaf that it performed with the metals. She then describes how you begin the cycle's new material by following a fruit tree through its seasonal changes.

You begin the conditioning cycle by taking the three deep breaths, performing the deepening exercises, and making the positive statements, and then you are deep in reverie. There is a tap on your left shoulder. You open your eyes. The instructor is leaning over and whispering, "Reach up and cut off one leaf, break it with your fingers, bring it to your nostrils, and mentally make an impression."

You may feel embarrassed, but you close your eyes and go through the motions. You do the same when she says that blossoms are appearing. Next, she says that small unripe fruit, then larger unripe fruit, and finally ripe fruit have appeared by turns. She then guides you mentally to your living room, where you face the south wall, project into the smaller leaf to make the four tests, and then project into the larger leaf. You open your eyes at the count of five.

The instructor is aware of the possibility that some students may have fallen asleep during the cycle. "Don't worry if you missed something," she says. "José Silva has given this training a large factor of safety, to use an engineering term—in fact, many times more strength than is actually needed."

She then asks the class to select a pet, a dog or cat you are familiar with. You select the dachshund owned by the friend into whose apartment you will be moving.

"We will set up physiological points of reference, because we know pets as a body. We will examine various organs, not by going inside these organs, but by looking at them from an external point of view. We will be seeing them mentally, though not in fact entering the animal's body. We will examine the skull, the brain, the lungs, the heart, the kidneys. By desiring to see them, we will project to their level and see them in any way we know them to be. This means that if you are not sure what, for example, a dog's liver looks like, you can imagine what it looks like based on your memory of, say, a calf's liver."

The conditioning cycle begins, and you make a mental trip through the body of the animal you've chosen. With each snap of the lecturer's fingers, you see another organ.

"If you used your dog," says the instructor, "you might find that dog extra affectionate when you get home tonight, as if to say, 'Now you are talking my language.' Cats are different; they value their privacy. Instead of rubbing up against your leg tonight when you get home, your cat may disappear under the couch."

After the break, the lecturer says that although the class has finally reached the top of the ladder in the evolution of matter and is ready to program subjective points of reference at the human level, there will first be two conditioning cycles devoted to creating a laboratory for creative, right-brain work. "In this left-brain world, we have special places for special activities—a kitchen to cook in, a dining room to eat in, an office to work in. We will do the same for the right brain now. We will create a laboratory in which to do our intuitive or psychic work."

"We will go to a deeper level this time—the creative level—with an extra 10-to-1 countdown. Then you will create a room—four walls, a ceiling, and a floor—and decorate it any way you wish. I'll give you plenty of time." She counts to 3 and snaps her fingers.

"Now we'll create a chair, a desk, a clock, a perpetual calendar, filing cabinets, tools, and equipment, and finally chemicals and medicines. For each, I will give you plenty of time." Again she counts to 3 and snaps her fingers.

Now the conditioning cycle is underway and you have arrived at the creative level. "Create the room that will be your laboratory." Mentally, you see a long room with an all-glass ceiling that permits you to observe the moon and stars at night. You also create a large oval window to your left so you can see the sunrise and another to your right where you know the sunset will be. Gold walls, white shag rug.

Your chair is comfortably padded and equipped with heating coils. Your desk is a V.I.P. model made of mahogany. A digital clock is built into the desk and a perpetual calendar, also digital, is operated by buttons on the chair's left arm. The filing cabinets are computerized—you push the buttons on the arm of your chair and the information you seek flashes on your desktop. Tools and medications pop out of the wall to your right just by your wanting them.

At the end of the cycle, each member of the class is invited to describe his or her laboratory. "I may want to steal some ideas for my own," warns the instructor.

You think yours is as futuristic as it can get. But by the time it is your turn, some of the others have described images so wildly imaginative they make yours seem conservative.

"In today's final conditioning cycle," continues the instructor, "we will install a screen on our laboratory's south wall. We will also create a compartmentlike elevator with a door that moves down into the floor. Its controls, too, are located on the arm of your chair. And we will use this compartment to introduce counselors."

She explains how an incident in José Silva's researching years led to the idea of counselors. His daughter Margarita, at about age seven, was working on a health case in her laboratory when she became agitated.

"What's wrong, dear?" asked José.

"Her eyes are big; she scares me" was the reply.

"Snap the fingers of your left hand and she'll get smaller," instructed José. He watched as Margarita did this, and soon she was smiling.

"How is it now?" José asked.

"She's like a small doll. She doesn't scare me."

José thought about this later. What if he had not been there? Maybe he should have his children create adults to be present in their laboratories, not as babysitters but as advisors or counselors. He followed through with his youngsters, and the idea worked out well. His youngsters each created a counselor and got advice in the laboratory just by asking. José was delighted.

"Ask your counselor what he thinks of my idea to create him," José had said to one of his children working on a problem in the laboratory.

"He says, 'What makes you think it was your idea in the first place?'" was the immediate answer, not exactly befitting a child.

Later, Margarita did not feel comfortable asking her male counselor to help with a female physiological problem. She told him to go away, and she brought in a female counselor. After that, José had his youngsters create a second counselor so there would be a male counselor present for male problems, and a female one for female problems.

The instructor tells you that you may select any male or female counselor from the present or the past or that you may create one. Never let a counselor appear spontaneously. When you reach that part of the conditioning cycle, you decide to make it happen. First, you select Albert Einstein, and he appears in your elevator compartment. Then you select Florence Nightingale, and she appears. Later, the other students share their counselors' identities. They range from "my mother" to Jesus.

On the way home, you stop in at your friend's apartment to confirm what furniture he will be leaving behind when he relocates. When he opens the door, the usually sedate dachshund is all over you, jumping, licking, wagging his tail, and jumping again.

"He is never like this!" exclaims your friend. "He must sense I'm giving him to the Humane Society and he's proclaiming that he wants to stay with you."

You wonder if there isn't another reason.

Chapter 17
The Silva Training:
Day 4

Before you leave your apartment Sunday morning to attend the fourth and final day of the training, you have homework to do. The lecturer has asked each student to bring three cases on separate pieces of paper. A case is the detailed description of a person you know to be sick.

Perhaps you list your father, who has been semiparalyzed by a stroke and is in a wheelchair. You write his name, address, age, and sex on one side of the paper, and a description of him and of his illness on the other side. The lecturer has explained that you will be giving the name, address, age, and sex to a fellow student, and that that student will then describe the person, detect the illness, and correct it.

Your second case is a friend who is now in the hospital recovering from injuries received in a car accident. Your third case is the chronic alcoholic in the apartment above you who beats his wife. You prepare the cases, but you may be filled with skepticism. Describe *and* cure a person you've never even heard of? This claim, you're thinking, goes too far.

"Please do not discuss your cases with anybody," the instructor is announcing as you enter. "Today we have only two more conditioning cycles and then the training will be complete. These will be devoted to setting up right-brain points of reference for the human kingdom. Even though you have set up these points of reference for the inanimate, vegetable, and animal kingdoms, you need to work first at the human level—your own kingdom— before you work on animal, plants, or inorganic matter. In fact, the human kingdom is the easiest kingdom to work with, since you are part of it. Crossing over to others is more difficult. And you need to start with the easiest level first, certainly not the hardest. Then, as you succeed and develop your expectations and beliefs, you will be able to cross into other realms—for example, to find out why plants are not growing or to discover mineral veins."

Your friend is nodding with understanding. You are next with a question.

"I can understand how we heal ourselves. Our mind controls our body. But how can we heal somebody else—at a distance?"

"You're psychic," replies the instructor. "I was just going to cover that."

Your friend turns around, looks at you, and smiles. It makes your day.

"Let's tackle this question of how it is possible to heal someone at a distance. Space is a characteristic of the material world perceived by the left brain. But in our healing we are using the right brain and are therefore functioning in the Creative Realm, where space is not a factor. You might say we transcend space, or that, when we are functioning through the right brain, space doesn't exist for us.

"As to how we are able to actually change or eliminate unwanted conditions in others, think about how you do this in your own body. Now realize that if there is no space, then there is no separation between minds. We are all as one. The energy of consciousness can be focused anywhere, can detect problems at a given energy level, and can make corrections at that energy level. The energy level is the *causal* level—the creative realm. And with the energy level changed, the physical level must follow. Go to your laboratory level, put a person in front of your Mental Screen, mentally detect a problem, see the person well, imagine fixing the problem—and you simply *create* the wellness.

"Remember, when you reach the count of one in this conditioning cycle, you will be in your laboratory. Greet your counselors and say a welcoming prayer with them. Realize that you are sharing a spiritual moment. If you pursue a religion, use its most powerful prayer so you can be certain you are aligning yourself with the highest creative powers. But if you are not used to praying or don't believe in it, follow your own spiritual guidance.

"At this point, if you have any doubts about your counselors, don't 'fire' them without cause. You know them to be geniuses. What cause could you have for firing a genius? Your attitude is the key. If you do not accept your counselors as geniuses and think they might make mistakes, they probably will. Before firing a counselor, try changing your own attitude—your expectation and belief—about the person."

It may occur to you that if you can correct illness, there is no reason to believe you will not live forever.

The instructor addresses this question directly. "Cells and organs tire and cease to replenish themselves vigorously, says José Silva, and therefore we cannot live forever. But, he points out, we can all die healthy."

Now the instructor asks each student to choose a partner— "somebody you know, whose face you can remember easily. You will use this person as your subject in these two conditioning cycles, setting subjective points of reference from a physiological point of view."

The instructor takes you through the three deep breaths, the three sets of three numbers, a 10-to-1 deepening countdown, the "genius statement," and the effective sensory projection statements.

"In a moment I am going to count from 10 to 1. You will enter the laboratory level and will meet your counselors, and the three of you will say a welcoming prayer."

When she reaches the count of 1, sure enough, you are there. You see your laboratory just as you created it. And there are Albert Einstein and Florence Nightingale. They seem to be in a prayerful attitude already. You join them. "Dear God, please help me succeed."

The friend you chose before the exercise began is now on your Mental Screen. You've examined the skull. Now you are examining the brain. "Recall your previous experience of how a brain looks. Desire to detect the various colors of the brain such as gray in the front, pink in the middle, and dark red in the back."

Mentally, you see the colors. The instructor is now drawing your attention to dark areas on the brain, which indicate brain damage. "To help correct this abnormality, erase the dark areas and project an impression of a healthy brain."

She takes you on a trip through the body, projecting to the

skeletal structure, the heart—even making it transparent—and the lungs. At each organ, she covers some of the problems that might exist and how they might be corrected. You come out on your own by thanking your counselors, saying a farewell prayer, and counting from 1 to 3. On opening your eyes, you snap your fingers, affirming that you are "wide awake, feeling great!"

In the last conditioning cycle of the day and of the training, you check out the stomach, intestinal tract, pancreas, liver, gall bladder, and kidneys. Each time, you are reminded of possible ailments and what you might do about them.

"Congratulations, class. You have outfitted your right brain hemisphere with all the points of reference it needs for making your intuition dependable. Have a good lunch."

After lunch, the lecturer asks the class to turn to page 73 in the manual and read "Directives for Orientologists." "Half the time this afternoon, you will be an orientologist—one who gives a case to the psychic. The other half of the time, you will be the psychic doing a case.

"As the orientologist giving a case, you will read this material to your psychic. Let's follow along as I go over it."

It seems simple enough. You ask your psychic to go to the laboratory level and give you a ready signal. You count backward from 10 to 1 to deepen. Then you give only the name, address, age, and sex. The two pages of instructions that follow contain a scanning-the-body procedure and ways to encourage the psychic to keep talking during the investigation. Before ending the session, the psychic makes corrections in the problems detected and "hits" are reviewed to reinforce the awareness of how it feels to be correct. The psychic then thanks the counselor, and comes out, and the two discuss the case.

"We will form groups of twos and threes. The third person can act as an observer, but all three will take turns being psychic or orientologist."

The groups form and position themselves around the room.

"I guess I'm the psychic first," says your partner, the very student you most wanted to be with.

You select one of your cases and open your manual. The case happens to be your hospitalized friend. You begin to read.

"Enter your laboratory level by the 3-to-1, 10-to-1 method. Let me know when you are ready . . . "

In a minute, your friend is ready. You give the name, age, address, and sex of your case. "At the count of 3, the body of this person will be on your screen." You count to 3 and snap your fingers. You repeat the name, age, address, and sex, and ask your psychic to scan the body.

The instructor has warned the class that, at least at first, a psychic will be reticent at speaking up. She turns out to be absolutely right. Your friend just sits there.

You read from the manual: "Keep talking as you investigate. Tell me everything you are inclined to say. You may feel as though you are making it up. This is the correct feeling."

"In bed. Broken leg."

"Which one?" you ask.

"Left."

"What else do you detect?" You have now put down the manual and are ad-libbing.

"Bandages, bruises. He must have been beaten up or been in an accident."

You are amazed. "Yes, you're right. Would you like to begin correcting whatever problems you see?"

A period of silence. Your friend's hands are moving as if sewing, applying medication, adjusting. "I'm finished. He'll be okay."

"Before you come out, let me say you have been totally correct. It was a car accident." You pick up your manual and start reading again. "Every time you enter this dimension with the sincere desire to help humanity, you will be helping yourself; your talents will increase, and you will become more accurate every time. And this is so.

"Thank you. You may thank your counselors, say the farewell prayer, and come out 1-to-10, 1-to-3 in perfect health."

You put the manual down and wait. When your friend's eyes open, you say, "You were fantastic. Just one thing. It is the right leg, not the left."

"Oh, it was to my left. So I said the left."

You shake your head in disbelief and can only repeat, "Fantastic."

Your friend opens the manual and pulls out a case. You realize it is your turn. Your friend begins to read. You go to your laboratory level. "I'm ready." "At the count of 3, the body of Charlotte Keith, age sixty-six, of Thomas, Tennessee, will be on your screen."

You hear the fingers snap. You see a form. It is not too clear. How can you possibly detect a physical problem? You scan the body. Zilch. Hey, Charlotte, what's the problem? you ask mentally. Your attention is called to the chest area. Are those spots on her lungs? You report to your friend and explain that you will fix up Charlotte by cleaning up the spots. You erase them. You see her lungs, and they are perfect. "Okay, I'm coming out."

"Wait," says your friend, "you are right about the lungs. She has a bad, chronic cough. But she also has severe arthritis in her fingers. Before you come out, please make a correction there, too."

You wipe her fingers, ridding the joints of a fine powder that you now see. You thank your counselors, say a prayer, and count yourself up.

Your friend wears a broad grin. "You were great!"

"I don't believe it."

Your friends show you the paper. It's true. Now you have to believe it.

You feel a great relief. You are a psychic, a clairvoyant.

"Why do you think I missed the arthritis?" you ask your friend.

"You were probably as nervous as I was and wanted to get it over with."

It sounds like a reasonable explanation. Next your friend goes to the laboratory level. You give your father. "He can't walk. Brain problem." She works on his brain.

Your next case as a psychic is a young girl with severe acne. She would not face you, so you guess the problem. You manifest an acne cream and fix her up.

When all the cases have been completed by all the groups, the lecturer asks the class to rearrange the chairs and reconvene.

Counselors brag about their psychics. Your friend tells how

well you did. You tell how well your friend did. Everybody in the class had some measure of success. Certificates of completion are awarded; they are signed by the lecturer and by José Silva. Also, identification cards are handed out that enable participants to recycle free of charge anytime, anywhere in the world.

The training is over. Graduates mill about. Nobody wants to leave. The lecturer is bestowed with kisses and embraces from males and females alike. Addresses and phone numbers are exchanged. You cannot remember ever feeling such exhilaration.

The next day, when you awake in the morning, you lie in bed thinking about what it all means. There is one missing link. You lean over, pick up the phone, and dial your parents' number.

Your mother answers. "How was your workshop, dear?"

"Great," you reply. "How's dad?"

"You won't believe this, but last night he got up from his wheelchair, took one step, and changed the television channel!"

"I believe it, Mom. Now you should get him one of those gadgets to lean on and help him walk."

"That's what I'm going out to do later this morning."

Next you phone your friend to relate the "miracle." Your friend has not yet had a chance to follow up on your healing work. "I'll call you later."

You hang up. You close your eyes, go to alpha level, and program for a perfect day.

Chapter 18
Ten Silva Steps to Improve the World

As stated earlier, this book does not teach you to be a clairvoyant. It is a book *about* the training rather than a training book. However, it offers you the opportunity to take the first steps toward gaining control of your life and beginning to improve the world for yourself and humankind as a whole. This chapter, therefore, represents a change of pace and tone. It is a how-to chapter, consisting of ten active steps you can take to begin your self-transformation.

Steps 1 through 3 are related to the training; steps 4 to 10, read and experienced in order, constitute a mini self-training manual. Note the use of the word *experienced*. Reading the pages will not be enough to train you. Putting the book down and doing the exercises is the key.

Step 1: If there is a Silva Mind Control listing in your telephone book, that means there is a Silva Method center and a Silva Method lecturer in your area. The Silva Mind Control Basic Lecture Series is a thirty-two to forty-hour experience of lectures and mental training exercises. It is usually given in a hotel or motel, if no permanent center exists in an area. It is fully guaranteed. If you are not satisfied at the completion of the seminar, your lecturer will refund your money. Also, when you complete the training, you will have the privilege of taking it again, free of charge, to reinforce your skills. You may take it at the same place from the same lecturer or you may take it anywhere in the country or in the world where it is given.

If there is no listing in your phone book, you can find out the location closest to you by contacting Silva headquarters.*

* Write, phone, telex, or FAX: Silva Mind Control International, P.O. Box 2249, Laredo, Texas 78044-2249. Phone: (512) 722-6391. Telex: 763328 Silva Mind Lar. FAX: (512) 722-7532.

The in-person training is the most effective approach to learning the method. However, if it is impossible to take the training, consider the next step.

Step 2: The publisher of this book is also the publisher of *You the Healer*, which presents a daily program of self-training. The course lasts forty days and, although the accent is on the applications of the Silva Method for health, the skills acquired can be applied generally for self-improvement and problem solving. *You the Healer* is by José Silva and Robert B. Stone and is available from H J Kramer Inc., P.O. Box 1082, Tiburon, CA 94920.

The key to the training, as provided in this how-to book, is a countdown exercise done right after awakening. For the first ten mornings, you count down from 100 to 1; the next ten, you count from 50 to 1; the third ten mornings, 25 to 1; and the fourth ten mornings, 10 to 1. You are then able to reach the alpha level quickly and easily by a simple, short 10-to-1 countdown. Next, you are taught how to achieve benefits using the alpha level.

The four-day in-person training is the best route to take. The forty-day self-training is the second-best route. The following seven steps constitute the third-best approach.

Step 3: You can begin a forty-day self-training course using the same morning countdowns described above. Follow these procedures:

When you awaken in the morning, go to the bathroom if you have to, so that when you return to bed you will be comfortable and relaxed.

Before returning to bed, set your alarm clock to ring in ten to fifteen minutes in case you fall asleep. Also, prop your pillows up so that you are not fully reclining. Once back in bed, close your eyes, turn them slightly upward toward your eyebrows, take a deep breath, and exhale. Breathe normally and begin to count down from 100, thinking at a pace of about one number per second. Do not count aloud. Count mentally to yourself, keeping your eyes closed.

When you reach 1, end your relaxation session in the following way: Tell yourself mentally, "I am going to count from 1 to 5.

When I reach 5, I will open my eyes, be wide awake, feeling fine, better than before." When you reach 3, mentally repeat that statement and continue counting. When you reach 5, open your eyes and repeat mentally, "I am wide awake, feeling fine, feeling better than before."

After ten mornings, count from 50 to 1. After ten more mornings, count from 25 to 1. Finally, on the last ten mornings, count from 10 to 1. By this time, you will probably produce the same deep state of relaxation with ten counts that a lengthy 100 to 1 countdown produced at the start. Perhaps you will go deeper. You will have learned to slow your brain waves, so you will now be able to go to the alpha level by closing your eyes, turning them slightly upward, taking a nice deep breath, exhaling, and counting backward from 10 to 1.

Just being at alpha is beneficial. Thinking that takes place at alpha is centered thinking, involving both brain hemispheres and providing increased answers, creativity, and wisdom. Steps 4 through 10 give you instructions on how to deepen your alpha level to make it more effective, and how to use it for specific benefits.

Step 4: Occasionally, you may want to add other steps to your morning countdown exercise in order to deepen your alpha level for greater effectiveness. Here are some deepening exercises to choose from. Use them after you have reached the count of 1.

- Perform progressive relaxation by concentrating on specific parts of your body and relaxing each part as you go. Start at your scalp. Relax it. Then move down through your forehead, eyes, face, mouth, and neck, relaxing each separately. Do the same for your torso—shoulders, chest, back, and hips. Finally, relax your thighs, knees, legs, feet, and toes. Take your time and enjoy it.
- Use an affirmation such as "Every time I relax this way I go deeper faster."
- Visualize some passive scenes that you can recall—a shady nook, a peaceful lake, a country lane. Make the mental pictures real; feel that you are there.

Step 5: Use the next six steps (5 through 10) at alpha. The success of these steps depends on how far along you are in Step 3 and how well you have applied Step 4 in deepening your alpha level. A satisfactorily deep alpha level opens your mind to be programmed like a computer. You can provide mental programming either with words or pictures. Always end your session with the 1 to 5 count-up explained in Step 3.

When you say the following mental affirmations one or more times at the alpha level, they will become living truth for you.

- Every day in every way I am getting better, better, and better.
- Positive thoughts bring me all the benefits and advantages I desire.
- I will always maintain a perfectly healthy body and mind.

It is best to start with one easily remembered affirmation. Only add another when you are sure you will not need to exert yourself to remember the thoughts, thereby ruining your relaxation.

You can compose your own affirmation to obtain positive personality or behavioral changes. They will work if you keep them (1) short, (2) believable, (3) positive, and (4) creative—to solve, not make, problems for yourself and others.

Step 6: Even before your fortieth morning, you will be relaxing deeply—deeply enough to use your alpha level to change unwanted feelings, attitudes, and even minor unwanted physical conditions. Adding one or two deepening techniques from Step 4 will enhance your relaxation further. Now you can program out unwanted conditions and program in the preferable condition. First, read the following procedure. Then, at any time, while you are relaxed, review it in your mind and affirm that the desired results will occur. When you open your eyes at the count of 5, the change will take place.

As an example, perhaps you are troubled by always being tired and sleepy on the job or driving a car. You can use Step 6 to correct this, either right at your desk or in your car—having pulled off the road and turned off the motor. Close your eyes, take a deep breath, count down from whatever morning number you are at. When you reach the count of 1, deepen your

level either by the progressive relaxation method or by visualiz-
ing a passive scene.

Then tell yourself mentally, "I am drowsy and sleepy. I don't
want to be drowsy and sleepy. I want to be wide awake, feeling
fine and in perfect health. I am going to count from 1 to 5. At
the count of 5, I will open my eyes, be wide awake, feeling fine
and in perfect health. I will not be drowsy and sleepy. I will be
wide awake." Count from 1 to 3, then stop and remind yourself, "At the count of 5, I will open my eyes, be wide awake,
feeling fine and in perfect health." Complete your count and
at the count of 5, open your eyes and reaffirm mentally: "I am
wide awake, feeling fine and in perfect health, feeling better than
before." And so you will be.

Many unwanted conditions are easily changed with this technique: tension headaches, the morning "blahs," morose feelings,
and negative attitudes. The basic procedure for all is the same:
Go to your alpha level, deepen, identify the unwanted condition, state what you want instead of it. Affirm that you will have
the wanted conditon when you open your eyes at the count of 5.
Remind yourself of this at the count of 3. Open your eyes at
the count of 5, reaffirming the arrival of the wanted condition.

Step 7: With the Silva Method, you can help not only yourself but other people as well. Step 7 is one method for helping
others. With this technique, without speaking a single word, you
can help children to stop wetting their beds or sucking their
thumbs. Or you can help adults rise to a more mature level of
understanding or attitude. Again, without speaking a single word,
you will be engaging in what is called subjective communication.

After regular conversation failed time after time, Mr. L. used
subjective communication to induce his neighbor to lower the
volume of his television set. Miss F. had a sulking boyfriend call
her. Mrs. S. got a child to be more motivated about homework.

To begin to engage in subjective communication, go to your
alpha level and deepen it as described in steps 3 and 4. At alpha
level, visualize the person you need to talk to and *mentally* speak
to the person. Identify the problem and suggest a solution. Then
end your session with the 1-to-5 count-up.

The form of the mental message you send is important. If you were dealing with trying to get a loud radio turned down, you would be wasting your time to say mentally, "You bum, turn that radio down or I'll call the police!" This sort of strong-arming might work at the objective level, but never at the subjective level.

At the subjective level, a right-brain function, your higher self is in touch with the other person's higher self. If you talk in a hostile way, you create a dichotomy or polarity. The right hemisphere is thus turned off, because polarity falls into the left brain's jurisdiction. So, using a willful, adversarial tone will only lead to failure. The secret is to frame your message in a loving way.

Also, if you take the tone that "I'm right and you're wrong" in your mental conversation, you will break your connection with the right brain, and for the same reason — duality is dealt with by the left brain. To succeed, avoid "who is right"; just stick to "*what is right.*"

To keep subjective communication on the loving, mutual basis that will enable it to succeed, your mental message might be, "My fine neighbor, a loud radio can eventually harm your hearing as well as jangle your neighbors' nerves. Wouldn't it be better for you and for me to lower it to a more mutually comfortable level?"

Step 8: You can adapt the Silva Method to help your doctor help you to relieve minor ailments. Here are the steps:

- Do your morning countdown exercise and deepen your relaxation (steps 3 and 4).
- Imagine that you are protecting your intelligence inside your body and actually go to the trouble spot.
- Correct the problem in whatever way comes to mind (sew it up, apply a healing balm, splint it, and so on).
- See the problem disappear. See yourself healthy. See the area working normally.
- End your session with the usual 1-to-5 count-up.

Here are some specific examples using the Silva Method to help self-healing take place:

- Visit your white blood cells. Urge them to rally to expel an invader. See the ensuing battle happening any way you wish.
- Visit your liver. Greet it lovingly. Suggest to it that a little less uric acid would be preferable. See the gout swelling disappear.
- Visit a sore back muscle. Apply an imaginary salve that heals sore back muscles. Visualize the back muscles as "grateful" and restored to painless normal.

Step 9: You can program yourself to go to a deeper level of awareness every time you put together the thumb and first two fingers of either hand. The further along you are in your progress as described in Step 3, the more effective this Three-Fingers Technique will be. Here's how to do it:

While at your deepened level in the morning exercise, put the three fingers of either hand together and mentally instruct yourself, "Every time I put together these three fingers of either hand, my mind functions at a deeper level of awareness." Repeat two more times and end your session in the usual 1-to-5 manner.

You have created a way to instantly activate more alpha brain-wave frequencies and thus more participation by the right brain. Whenever you need to be more aware, put your three fingers together. It will help you to

- make the right decision;
- say the right words;
- arrive at an optimum solution;
- do the wisest thing;
- act in an appropriate manner.

There are two ways to reinforce the Three-Fingers Technique. One, repeat the above programming from time to time. Two, prior to using it to gain a specific benefit, go to alpha level and program it to accomplish the specific task. Do this by adding to the above programming, for example, "so that I will say the right thing at this afternoon's meeting for the company's maximum benefit."

Step 10: To gain control of your well-being and guarantee your success, it is necessary to leave behind problem-oriented thinking and adopt *solution*-oriented thinking. Since relaxed thinking is creative, problem thinking reinforces problems, but solution thinking brings about solutions.

Make the change by using the Silva technique called the Mirror of the Mind. Prepare to use this technique by going to your deepened level during one morning exercise and imagining a mirror. Imagine that the mirror can encompass a scene of any size. Also imagine that the frame of this mirror can be changed from blue to white. Explain to yourself that the blue frame will denote the problem and the white frame will denote the solution or the goal that you want to reach.

Once you have created the Mirror of the Mind at a morning session, you will be able to use it at any time. Here are the steps for doing so:

- Do your morning exercise and deepen your relaxation (steps 3 and 4).
- Visualize the blue-framed mirror as reflecting the problematic object, people, or scene, and make a study of the problem.
- Erase this image, move the mirror slightly to your left, mentally change the frame from blue to white, and "see" the solution attained or the goal reached.
- Remind yourself that from now on, whenever you think of this project, you will see it as the solution framed in white.
- End your session with the usual 1-to-5 count-up.

Moving the mirror to the left denotes a time shift slightly into the future. Step 4 is the key; it moves you in the direction of thinking positively. And positive thinking brings you all the benefits and advantages you desire.

Once you have completed Step 3, you can close your eyes, take a deep breath, count from 10 to 1, and apply positive thinking anytime, anywhere, for any constructive, creative, or problem-solving purpose. You will be thinking with both hemispheres. Your left brain provides you with a visible means of support in this material world. Now, thanks to your right brain, you will also have an invisible means of support.

Chapter 19
Glimpses of a Silva Future

José Silva has come a long way from sweeping out a barbershop to leading millions to a better life. Looking back, we see no manger, no donkey, no crucifixion. But we do see a "solitary life" bringing about miracles.

The purpose of this chapter, however, is not to create a parallel between Jesus and José, but rather to point to the implications of the latter's work in the decade ahead. I take a purely subjective approach here. José has already given his glimpses of the future in *You the Healer*. The future he painted there embraced the following Silva-oriented innovations:

- Human beings will all die healthy, without suffering the health problems we now identify with old age.
- Executives will make use of their activated intuition and clairvoyance to reach correct business decisions.
- Students graduating will be intuitively drawn to the jobs for which they are best suited and that best serve the needs of humanity in their particular places and times.
- People will be more humane, exhibiting more respect for all forms of life.
- Natural resources will be used more efficiently, and alternative sources will be clairvoyantly discerned and located.
- Labor and management will communicate subjectively and work together for the common good.
- Personnel directors will be better at hiring the right people for the right jobs, financial counselors will be more accurate in investment decisions, and industrialists will know what to manufacture and in what quantities.
- Government leaders will be wiser and more statesmanlike, fostering peace and happiness on earth.

Together, these predictions represent a visionary's approach to the future. José can function from that height; for me, the atmosphere there is too rarefied. I prefer a mere bird's-eye view.

What follows is my own perception of our direction and our possible future.

We are witnessing a major shift in human understanding here on earth. For centuries, we have been content with a mechanical view of nature, life, and the universe. Period.

The period is being replaced with a plus sign. And after the plus sign comes consciousness. Scientific researchers have traditionally ignored human consciousness, even though their consciousness has affected the outcomes of their experiments.

Acknowledging and measuring the effect of human consciousness on research can be complicated. But including consciousness as a subject of study in itself represents a raising of that consciousness. It shows a movement toward the spiritual and the divine. The study of consciousness moves us toward our own creative source, the understanding and tapping of which have been science's greatest challenge.

As the Silva Method gradually removes the blinders from humankind so that educators, scientists, and healers begin to use consciousness as a creative tool, a fundamental truth emerges: Stated succinctly, consciousness affects matter.

Right now, the Silva Method is teaching individuals to change their personal worlds. Silva practitioners are transforming sick organs into healthy ones, sick bank balances into healthy ones, sick relationships into healthy ones. Our glimpse into the future reveals collaboration between large numbers of people trained to do these things. Through cooperative relaxation and visualization, the practitioners of the future could — will! — work on changing sick cultures, sick international relationships, and sick environments into healthy counterparts.

In Japan's tradition, it is said that "the greatest warrior conquers himself first." The Silva Method has started with the individual. The next step is the group.

In September 1989, an education summit was held in Charlottesville, Virginia, to set national goals for American education and form a national Governors' Association Task Force on Education to give input toward these goals. Included among these goals were strengthening the problem-solving and thinking skills of all students, developing positive attitudes and self-concepts in children, and improving the level of learning to guarantee a competitive work force.

What a coincidence! These also happen to be not only the goals of the Silva Method but also its very accomplishments.

As a consciousness-based paradigm eases itself into scientific circles, it eases itself into educators' circles, politicians' circles, and health-care circles. And it thus becomes revealed that there was always one circle.

What does the injection of consciousness into science, education, and politics mean to individuals? It means that we will gradually begin to understand how fully subjective human experience counts in shaping our styles of life. We will daydream more. We will draw more heavily on the creative source within us (which is really outside us — all around us — too) to solve our problems. We will all rise to a new level of mutual respect and harmony. We will be more in tune with nature and the environment.

And as we change, we will change history.

Wait a minute, you say. This sounds pretty visionary itself — way above a "bird's-eye" view.

No, I reply. I went to my relaxed level and wrote it all at alpha.

Expectation and belief have been vital ingredients for success with the Silva Method. As the years go by and more and more "miracles" are documented, the ingredients of expectation and belief begin to build on themselves.

These ingredients are now understood to be so important that even the behaviorists are accepting their role in shaping the courses of our lives and our health. One of the world's leading experts on behavioral medicine, Dr. Neal Miller of Yale University and Rockefeller University, emphasizes that the placebo response is proof that thoughts and expectations can affect physiological reality. Another example of expanding acceptance of the role of consciousness is brain surgeon Dr. Karl Pribram's observation that brain neurons create a hologram. Between these two examples lies the unmistakable fact that consciousness is coming of age.

One interesting creation story has it that the Creator chose to hide the secret of creation not on the highest mountain or under the deepest sea, where humans would find it easily, but within the human mind, the last place humans would look.

Jesus exhorted us to look there, but that part of his teaching was never fully grasped. Perhaps there were others after him, but none succeeded as well as José Silva, not only in effectiveness but also in sheer numbers. And numbers count.

It has been much easier for other researchers to ignore the work of José Silva than to explain it. It was the same with Jesus and it was the same with pioneering psychologist Carl Jung, who summed up his concept of the collective unconscious this way: "It is an extension that can reach anywhere . . . as we cannot say where the world ends, so we cannot say where the unconscious ends, or whether it ends anywhere."

After Jung, we can gain confirmation from physicist Erwin Schrödinger, generally accepted as one of the leading scientists of the century, whose study of waves are the basis of quantum mechanics. He said of the billions of human minds on earth, "The overall number of minds is just one."

Larry Dossey, M.D., former chief of staff of the Medical City Dallas Hospital and now an internist with the Dallas Diagnostic Association, describes how a patient of his suffered a cardiac arrest during gallbladder surgery but was successfully resuscitated. This patient later described things she "saw." She said the chief surgeon was wearing unmatched socks that day. She told the names of the surgeons awaiting their next case down the hall in the surgeon's lounge. She listed the upcoming cases as posted on the blackboard. All of this was completely accurate. But even more astonishing was the fact that this patient was congenitally blind and had never seen anything in her life.*

Talk about the power of the mind! You are in the vanguard, as an appreciation of and fascination with consciousness begins to grip today's thinkers. You know the power of the mind. You may not yet have developed your mental power fully, but you have

* *Recovering the Soul: A Scientific and Spiritual Search* (New York: Bantam, 1989).

enough belief in it now to allow this story of a blind patient's clear vision to rest comfortably in your memory.

Gratifyingly, the percentage of other people who will sweep that case out of their sight is decreasing. Skeptics may still be in the majority, but the margin is shrinking. "Miracles" such as the ones that the Silva Method generates are becoming more and more acceptable to the masses. Nevertheless, the rate at which this appears to be happening is slower in the more materialistic West than in developing countries or in the East, where either less materialism or more spiritual awareness prevails. This means that, in the future, the Silva Method may have a broader foreign base and eventually its deserved place in planetary society.

Where do you fit into this rising tide of expanding consciousness? A certain man has the answer—the man who tapped the secrets of the human mind.

If you are already a graduate of the Silva Method, you are probably already helping to turn the tide by using the power of consciousness. If you have a problem to solve, you order a dream to give you the answer or you use the Glass-of-Water Technique to effect a solution. If there is an end result you want to attain or a goal you want to reach, you use the Mirror of the Mind to program for it. If you have a business choice to make, you go to your laboratory level and let your counselors help you. If you or a dear one is taken with an illness, again you go to your laboratory and "fix" the problem, seeing the abnormality fade and normality resume. If there is an immediate need for geniuslike action on your part, you put your three fingers together. All of these approaches, and the multitude available through the full course of training, trigger both more of your mind and the larger Mind to which it is connected to go to work for you.

If you are not so trained, you are not in full control. You are a candidate for success *or* failure, health *or* disease, happiness *or* unhappiness. Because you do not have the skill to use the full power of your mind, you may have a visible means of support, but you have little if any invisible means of support. You are like a ship without a rudder. You may think you are going places, but you are really drifting on the open sea.

Whatever we are doing that is right is only a small fraction of what we could be doing and should be doing. Why? Because we are using only a fraction of our minds, and the part we are not using is the most creative part.

Is the answer to be sought in town hall meetings, national conclaves, or international conferences?

No. There is another place you must go.

Are you willing to go to the kingdom within and activate more of your mind?

I hope your answer is yes.

José Silva hopes your answer is yes.

About the Author

Robert B. Stone, Ph.D.,
is the author and coauthor of
more than seventy-five self-help books.
He is a Silva Method lecturer, has circled
the globe twice speaking on the powers of the
mind, and has launched Silva Mind Control
in Japan, New Zealand, and Thailand. He
was elected to the New York Academy
of Science and is a member
of MENSA.

You may want to learn more about the amazing Silva Method or work with a Silva Method lecturer in developing your skill. The Silva Mind Control Basic Lecture Series is a thirty-two-hour experience of lectures and mental training exercises that can change every minute of the rest of your life. It is guaranteed; if you are not satisfied at the completion of the seminar, your lecturer will refund your money.

The Silva Mind Control Basic Lecture Series can help you learn to

- take charge of your life;
- free the energy of your mind;
- enjoy superior health and vitality;
- master inner resources;
- continue to learn and grow;
- increase your earning power;
- become a superior human being.

The Silva Mind Control Basic Lecture Series is available across the United States and in seventy-nine countries worldwide. For further information, including the location closest to you, write, phone, telex, or FAX:

Silva Mind Control International, Inc.
P.O. Box 2249
Laredo, TX 78044-2249
United States of America
Phone: (512) 722-6391
Telex: 763328 Silva Mind Lar.
FAX: (512) 722-7532

BOOKS THAT TRANSFORM LIVES
FROM H J KRAMER INC

YOU THE HEALER:
THE WORLD-FAMOUS SILVA METHOD ON
HOW TO HEAL YOURSELF AND OTHERS
by José Silva and Robert B. Stone
*YOU THE HEALER is the complete course in
the Silva Method healing techniques presented
in a do-it-yourself forty-day format.*

WAY OF THE PEACEFUL WARRIOR
by Dan Millman
Available in book and audio cassette format
A tale of spiritual adventure . . . a worldwide best-seller!

SEVENFOLD PEACE: BODY, MIND, FAMILY,
COMMUNITY, CULTURE, ECOLOGY, GOD
by Gabriel Cousens, M.D.
*"This book expands our awareness of the dimensions of peace so
that we can all work effectively to create a world at peace."*
—JOHN ROBBINS, Author, *Diet for a New America*

An Orin/DaBen Book
OPENING TO CHANNEL:
HOW TO CONNECT WITH YOUR GUIDE
by Sanaya Roman and Duane Packer, Ph.D.
*This breakthrough book is the definitive
step-by-step guide to the art of channeling.*

An Orin/DaBen Book
CREATING MONEY
by Sanaya Roman and Duane Packer, Ph.D.
*"To be considered required reading for those who
aspire to financial well-being."*—BODY MIND SPIRIT

PURE LOVE:
AFFIRMATIONS JUST FOR THIS MOMENT
by Carole Daxter
*A very special book that affirms our connection
to a safe and friendly universe.*

LOVE AND PEACE THROUGH AFFIRMATION
by Carole Daxter
*"Among the leaders in books that inspire and expand human
awareness."*—COLIN SISSON, Author, *Rebirthing Made Easy*

TALKING WITH NATURE
by Michael J. Roads
*"Reads like a synthesis of Walden and
The Secret Life of Plants."*—EAST WEST JOURNAL

BOOKS THAT TRANSFORM LIVES
FROM H J KRAMER INC

ORIN BOOKS
by Sanaya Roman
*The Earth Life Series is a course in learning to
live with joy, sense energy, and grow spiritually.*

LIVING WITH JOY, BOOK I
*"I like this book because it describes the way I feel about
so many things."*—VIRGINIA SATIR, Author, *Peoplemaking*

PERSONAL POWER THROUGH AWARENESS:
A GUIDEBOOK FOR SENSITIVE PEOPLE, BOOK II
"Every sentence contains a pearl. . . ."—LILIAS FOLAN

SPIRITUAL GROWTH:
BEING YOUR HIGHER SELF, BOOK III
*Orin teaches how to reach upward to align with the
higher energies of the universe, look inward to expand
awareness, and move outward in world service.*

JOURNEY INTO NATURE
by Michael J. Roads
*"If you only read one book this year, make that book
JOURNEY INTO NATURE."*—FRIEND'S REVIEW

MESSENGERS OF LIGHT: THE ANGELS' GUIDE TO
SPIRITUAL GROWTH
by Terry Lynn Taylor
*At last, a practical way to connect with the angels
and to bring heaven into your life!*

EAT FOR HEALTH:
FAST AND SIMPLE WAYS OF ELIMINATING
DISEASES WITHOUT MEDICAL ASSISTANCE
by William Manahan, M.D.
*"Essential reading and an outstanding
selection."*—LIBRARY JOURNAL

AMAZING GRAINS: CREATING VEGETARIAN MAIN
DISHES WITH WHOLE GRAINS
by Joanne Saltzman
*AMAZING GRAINS is really two books in one, a book of recipes
and a book that teaches the creative process in cooking.*

JOY IN A WOOLLY COAT:
GRIEF SUPPORT FOR PET LOSS
by Julie Adams Church
*JOY IN A WOOLLY COAT is about living with,
loving, and letting go of treasured animal friends.*